Pennie Mu...

The Circle of Life

*Learn to love yourself and embrace
every relationship as a gift*

The Circle of Life – Learn to love yourself and embrace every relationship as a gift
©Pennie Munslow

ISBN: 978-1-906316-88-4

Published in 2011 by HotHive Books, Evesham, UK.
www.thehothive.com

The right of Pennie Munslow to be identified as the author of this work has been asserted by her in accordance with the Copyright, Designs and Patents Act 1988.

A CIP record of this book is available from the British Library.

Printed in the UK by Webmart, London.

Printed on paper from responsible sources.

Dedication

I dedicate this book to the three male role models in my life,
my Grandfather Luke Fletcher, my Father Ken Sperring
and last but not least to my husband Geoff for all the adventures
and learning he has introduced me to and for his steadfast love
and support against all odds.

Acknowledgements

I would like to thank my family, my friends and everyone whose path has crossed mine for the invaluable experiences that they have brought about for me. Each one in their own special and unique way has shown me the meaning of Truth, Freedom, Beauty and Love (even if I didn't appreciate it at the time!), culminating in the book and making me the person I am at this present moment in time. Thank you from the bottom of my heart.

About the Author

In 1969 I became an articled clerk to a firm of chartered surveyors, auctioneers and estate agents at a time when this was a male-dominated profession. I was the only girl at college, the first female articled clerk at the firm and, according to the local papers, "The First Female Auctioneer in the West Midlands."

My work involved me meeting people of all walks of life and opening my eyes to situations I hadn't appreciated existed. It exposed me to the different energies that can be felt in properties and on land and developed my desire to work with these energies to bring about healing where it is needed.

I feel that this is hugely important as Mother Earth needs all the rebalancing, retuning and energy healing that she can get. Whenever we are inspired, I and others make regular pilgrimages to places where there are buildings, monuments and land. There we reconnect energetically to the Earth's grid and re-energise her and all that is connected to her.

I found that in my work my masculine energy was very strong as it worked well with my business ethics and supported me generally in what was mainly a male-dominated world.

For a time I forgot about the creative side of me that had loved music, art, poetry and literature. Then as time went by I remembered this other side of myself, my feminine energy, and embraced it, learning how to balance the two.

As part of this I started looking at my relationships, especially the one with myself, in a completely different way. In certain circumstances I had considered myself a victim and this new way of thinking stopped me from feeling like that. I realised that I was responsible for everything that happened to me, which led me to recognise that I was in control of my life – something I found very empowering.

Because of this I now own who I am, and have brought the two sides of my life together. I am totally comfortable that I am a surveyor, business woman, holistic workshop facilitator, energy healer and Earth healer. Life is so much more special and I feel complete because of this wonderful balancing of energies. While on an adventure in New Zealand, I decided that

I wanted to share this enlightenment with others so that they too could empower themselves, as so many people I knew were having emotional relationship issues. I determined I would write about it and allow the words, like energy, to flow across the page. The Circle of Life is the end result…

If you need any help or advice along your journey then you are welcome to contact me at pennie@thecircleoflife.co. You can also follow my blog or website www.thecircleoflife.co for more inspiration.

Love

Pennie

Table of Contents

Land of Mystery

As the heat of the morning sun
Touches the water of the lake
Chilled by the winter night's cold air,
A mist hovers just above the surface
Making it look like a giant witches' cauldron.

Mist lingers in the valleys,
Creating the appearance of a large bush fire
Or a mysterious magical area
From whence some mythical creature
Duly emerges, to stamp its mark on the land.

New Zealand, Aotearoa, The Land of The Long White Cloud,
Use whichever name is appropriate for you.
This is the place where the day begins,
Where the Millennium started,
Where things are never as they seem.

The lake is a crater created by Mother Earth
When she shouted her needs to the world,
The heat of her love from her inner core
Erupted and flowed, changing the landscape for ever.
But did anyone listen? – no they did not.

The beautiful mountain covered in snow,
Where cries of pleasure are heard
From those enjoying the pleasure of winter sports,
Is a volcano in disguise, hiding the inner torment
Heart wrenching felt by Mother Earth.

There are places where mud bubbles and splutters,
Hot water screams from the Earth forming pools,
Steam escapes through cracks in the rocks,
Mountains appear as if from nowhere overnight
Watched by a million bright stars in the sky.

As you journey through each day
Acknowledge the beauty of where you are,
The singing of the birds, whisper of the wind,
Roar of the ocean as it obeys the moon,
Honour the mystery of this special land.

A Beginning

It is true greatness to have in one the frailty of a man
and the security of a god.

Seneca (3 BC–65 AD)

*T*his book, like me, was conceived in the UK. It was, however, written in New Zealand, in the east, where the global day begins and where there is much spiritual essence and mystery in its landscape and diverse spiritual belief in its people. The inhabitants of these islands treat differing beliefs with respect, so none is stifled or forced to practise in secret. This is as it should be in a land which seeks to uphold peace and freedom for all.

It was my wish for this book, which I have been inspired to write, to journey by following the pathway of the Sun to America, concluding in the west where the global day ends. I felt that would give a completeness which otherwise I may not have been able to attain. This aspiration, however, was not to be realised. Maybe if I am intended to write a further book, it will be appropriate for my wish to be brought about at that time. As it is, I have concluded my writing when the Moon is full and lights up the mysteries of the night sky, so in a sense I have completed the circle by starting with the strong, vibrant energy of the Sun and finishing with the gentle but powerful energy of the Moon.

My pathway, like that of everyone else I have spoken to and shared my life with, has not been an easy one. But through my adventures and experiences, and through meeting life's challenges and pain, I have grown as a person. So if, in deciding to share with you some of that knowledge, my words only help one person, giving them cause to think and subsequently change their mindset, then my time writing this book will have been spent wisely.

I have also been emotionally stirred by various relationships and situations to write poems, and have interspersed the sections of prose with some of them, thereby giving time to pause and reflect on whatever appeals to you most strongly. It is a book for you to dip into where you choose, going where it feels right for you to be. The order is not important. You might choose to close your eyes and just let the book fall open; or you might look at the different headings in the table of contents and choose that way. Of course, you might start at the beginning and read to the end. It is here to encourage and support you in processing any emotional issues, either with regard to yourself or with regard to another. The book can become your guide as you struggle to deal with internal issues that you have manifested in your outer reality, causing you to observe them and then address them. It can also be used as a map to help you understand the signposts that have been there but that you haven't noticed. However, as in the circle of the title, there is no real beginning and no real end – there is only where we are at any given moment in time, so be guided by whatever is appropriate for you.

This book is a key to unlocking parts of yourself of whose existence you are unaware (except at some deep subconscious level), liberating you and helping you to move forward with fewer mind-based restrictions and limitations. This attention to learning more about yourself, which is a work in progress, as you are, will cause fewer negative energies to manifest in your world – your outer reality – as you deal with your relationship issues. You – that is, your soul – are older than time. You already know all the wisdom and the truths of this amazing Universe deep down; you just need reminding of it and my book guides you on your way, helping you to connect with the flow of energy which is you and out of which everything in your world manifests.

Although it is written about my experiences and those of other women, please do not think that it is only meant to benefit females. Men share the same problems when we cut away the outer layers and reveal the true person beneath – the same insecurities, the same doubts and the same lack of self love.

So now, with great love from myself to the reader, I welcome you and invite you to read about self love, the ability to actually love yourself and feel completely at peace with this, becoming whole and seeing the effect of this on your life and on others who share it with you, even total strangers.

I have been blessed with the ability to channel wisdom from mystical energies, non-physical teachers. Their wisdom, which they wished to be included in the book, is at the end of each chapter, written in italics to differentiate it from my words. I don't know who they are but their energies are very special. They are highly evolved and are neither masculine nor feminine as their energies have blended into a perfect balance, making them androgynous. They have no names as they have no labels, for although it may be simpler for us to call them by a name, it would immediately impose restrictions and limitations on them because, as human beings, we would instantly have preconceived ideas. When I first started channelling knowledge, I stated that I only wanted to work with the highest energies that my physical body could carry and that I wanted to receive their wisdom, special knowledge and guidance. They have always honoured this request.

I would like to share a quote from New Zealander Barry Brailsford, author of a book entitled *Song of the Whale*, which I feel sums up the role of the writer beautifully:

"The writer is like water, with a memory that runs deep and wide. Everything comes from all that went before. It is of the beginning and all who gifted their life forward to give power to the pen. Thus the work breathes life. If the patterns run true they are of a universal mind and carry a message and beauty, which is of that realm. It is of creation and carries the vision that helps us take the dream forward. It is the essence of creativity. It is of the wairua, the spirit that moves."

Who Am I?

Am I a receptacle for food, a tumbler for drink?
A recipient of sound, a gourmet of taste
A sensor of touch, a submitter of noise
A conscious awareness of smell?
Am I someone's granddaughter, someone's daughter,
Someone's mother, someone's wife, someone's friend?
How do they all see me?
Do they see different facets of my personality
Which when joined together make a whole?

I am happy, I am sad
I am angry, I am calm
I am bitter, I am sweet
I am bad, I am good
I am a friend, I am an enemy
I am loyal, I am deceitful
I am truthful, I am a liar
I like myself, I hate myself
I am loving, I am cold
I like to be with people, I want to be alone
I have morals, I am immoral
I am gentle, I am vicious
I am caring, I don't care
I remember, I am forgetful
I am kind, I am rough
I am fair, I am unjust
I try hard, I don't bother
I am a success, I am a failure
I have friends, I am alone
I am loved, I am unloved
I am confident, I lack confidence
I am a believer, I have doubts

I have a soul which needs spiritual truth

I appreciate God's beautiful world
I am God's child
I have to take my own responsibility and accept my own destiny

I am ME

Who We Are

Nothing in life is to be feared, it is only to be understood.
Now is the time to understand more, so that we may fear less.

Marie Curie

At some stage in our life there is love, whether it be in the beginning, during or throughout life, or at the end. We always look to others when the word love is used – how much we love them and how much they love us. We very rarely consider how much we love ourselves. Indeed, normally when we think about ourselves our thoughts are generally negative – I'm too fat, I'm too thin, I'm ugly, my hair is too short/long/straight/curly or the wrong colour, I'm stupid/thick/ignorant. Basically I'm not loveable. If, however, my hair, face, nose, intelligence etc were right then I'd be perfect! Wrong. Because then we would find something else amiss with ourselves – if only I had lots of money/a house in the country/a yacht/my own business my life would be perfect! Wrong again. Until we realise that our emptiness, our lack of self worth, our lack of self fulfilment is because we don't love ourselves, the circle will continue and round we go again thinking that if only we had this/that our life would be ideal. Then briefly, when we achieve what we think we really want, we are happy for a very short period of time until the same old dissatisfaction hits us once more.

So what causes this dissatisfaction with ourselves and subsequently with our lives? Why this continual searching to find something better which we think will make us happy but which, in reality, is only a short-term fix? Why is it easier to complain about what we don't have rather than realising how really lucky we are? Why can't we be grateful for our positive attributes rather than running ourselves down by focusing on what we consider to be our lack of them? Do you recognise any of this behaviour in yourself? If not, you are one of the lucky few who totally love themselves and are completely connected with all the positive energies on this wonderful Planet. But for us others, each day brings its own challenges and yet again brings to our attention our general discontent with life. Indeed we are so busy being unhappy that we miss all the beautiful gifts and surprises that are given to us each day, whether they are smiles from strangers or wonderful Sunsets.

I was lucky as I was brought up by positive parents who instilled in me the belief that I was capable of doing and achieving anything I wanted. Despite this start in my life I have still been beset by negativities, self doubt and lack of self love. How much more difficult my life would have been if I had grown up in a negative household! However, like so many other parents, mine were anxious that I did not grow up to be vain or selfish. My positive attributes, therefore, were not highlighted, whereas my shortcomings were, so that I could concentrate on them and improve myself. It was a worthy decision by my parents to bring me up in this way and fitting for the time, which was only a few years after the end of the Second World War when there was still so much scarcity. They were just grateful to be alive and wanted the best for their offspring. But because of the way it was done – and not, I hasten to add, only by my parents – we were not allowed to dwell on our successes and on what made us feel good. We were always made to feel that we could do better and must try harder. One of my friends tried to attain perfection to please her father. Of course, it was impossible for her to achieve this so she always felt unsuccessful and has carried this into her adult life despite becoming a very successful person.

It is necessary to help a child grow and develop their skills. If, however, while the child is trying hard to improve they are never told what a wonderful, special, unique person they are, the child will continually feel second best and keep running themselves down. I recall an instance at school when a friend informed me that I had beautiful eyes. I knew that they were among my best features because others had said this before. So when she told me, I just said "I know." She was horrified at my reaction and thought I was being really conceited. I should have thanked her for the compliment before I said I knew, but with hindsight I could see that her parents, too, had impressed on her the importance of not being vain or conceited. I was not intentionally being either of those: I was merely acknowledging something about myself that I knew to be true.

If I had played a piece of music on the piano extremely well it would have been considered inappropriate for me to have said so, even though it was true. Since I would obviously know whether I had played the piece well or badly, why would it have been acceptable for me to say how badly I had played the piece but not for me to say how well I had played it? You can see the contradictions that our society has placed on us. Whether the piece was played well is a fact and cannot be disputed. In the same manner it was a matter of fact that I had beautiful eyes. It is not a question of being vain; it is a question of being honest and accepting your good points as well as your bad ones and loving yourself regardless.

Of course there is always room for improvement. If we had not continued our search for learning we might still be living in caves. But in this quest we must not make the mistake of thinking we are less than we are and therefore becoming dissatisfied with our lives. At any time in our evolution we are beautiful beings worthy of self love and if in our learning process we make mistakes, it is not for us to chastise ourselves. It is for us to learn from this experience and put our new-found knowledge to beneficial use.

Many of the words we use to reprimand ourselves are the same words that our parents used to tell us off when we were children. We must remember that we are no longer children, and therefore must stop treating ourselves like this. While it may have been inappropriate for us to behave in a certain way as a child this is not necessarily correct now that we are adults. So next time you admonish yourself consider what you are saying and whose words they are. If they are your parents' words and are no longer valid to you as an adult, address the situation, change the words and make them positive and self loving. Keep doing this until the time comes when you are no longer repeating the old pattern of scolding.

We are also very good at being judgemental about ourselves and others. We are continually saying – "we're not very good at that," "we could have done better," "we should have done this," "we should have done that," but all the time we are behaving in this way we are putting unnecessary pressure on, and making damaging judgements about, ourselves. We should also remember that there are times when we shock ourselves by acting in a way that is completely alien to us. Then we hope that others will not condemn us and we feel such relief if people do not pass judgement. When we are not being judged it is easier for us to address the situation, learn from it and move forward. We should remember this when we pass judgement on others. After all we don't know the pathways of their lives, just as they don't know ours, or where they are coming from or going to, or what experiences they need to have.

The Universe always tests me when I make any judgements of others. In the past I have made negative generalisations about people who are different from me without knowing them or anything about them. I think in many cases my comments were fear-based because of our differences. However, when the Universe brings such people into my life it gives me the opportunity to get to know them and their challenges and to realise that, whatever their colour, nationality, height or sexual persuasion, they are souls dealing, in some cases, with horrendous difficulties to the best of their ability. I am proud to count them among my friends.

It is a person's behaviour or their spoken words which cause us to react. If we are uncomfortable or angry because it is not what we want to hear or we feel that they have behaved in an inappropriate way, it is important that we hold back on our initial reactive thoughts. The reason is that we need to consider the real cause of our reaction by going beyond the surface of our initial response and looking deeper. You will discover, if not immediately, that there is a lesson here for you to learn. It is reminding you of a part of yourself that you don't like because you have failed to deal with issues surrounding this part of yourself. When you have addressed the situation you are always tested to see if there has been a complete clearing of the outstanding challenge. If a similar set of circumstances arises and you no longer respond as you did previously then it has been resolved. If, however, you still react in a similar way then you know that there is more work to be done. Anger and fear are both triggers highlighting that you have an issue which you need to address. So embrace them and recognise them for what they are. They are like teachers showing you what you have to learn in order to pass your examination. They are showing you what you need to discover in order to improve the quality of your life, help you walk your pathway and enable your soul to heal as a result of your knowledge.

Another thing for you to consider is that, every now and then, someone will say things to you that do not affect you emotionally, but with which you disagree. The reason for this is that, without realising it, they are actually talking about themselves when they are speaking to you: they are describing what they see of the world and how it appears to them. These are their issues, not yours, which is why your emotions have not become involved. These situations are so valuable. They bring your attention to your own personal matters that you need to deal with and at the same time they show you issues that the other person has. However, I reiterate that the latter are not your challenges and therefore there is no need to have an emotional reaction to what is being said. Love yourself. Know that you are beautiful, that you are as perfect as you can be at this moment in time and that you will continue growing and becoming more perfect.

The role of woman is often that which creates a martyr. This is not what is intended but is what happens in many instances. It is because of the mothering, nurturing instinct that is part of her biological make-up but it is also her inbuilt wish to make those around her happy and if that is to her cost, well, so be it. For she gains much pleasure from giving and creating the right atmosphere and environment around herself and those for whom she cares. In the short term this is perfectly acceptable, but in the long term she becomes so used to going without that she loses her ability to decide when she wants something for herself. Indeed, she is so used to going without that she feels guilty about buying anything for herself. What happens in this scenario is that she either continues going without and subsequently making do, or she buys something for herself and feels so guilty that she cannot enjoy it for what it truly is. She considers what she could have spent that money on, such as food, clothes for the children, something for the house, a surprise for her husband or partner, and, whereas she considers that all this is acceptable, she does not realise that in all this giving to others she is doing very great harm to herself. She is repeating the pattern over and over again that she does not deserve to have good things for herself. She can accept these things from others but not from herself. She feels that in spending money on herself she is depriving those that she loves.

However, what she is not taking into account is that where originally her gifts to those in her family came from the point of love within her, now they come from obligation and guilt and therefore the energy of her gifts is no longer resonating with the purity that it once had. She in turn is becoming angry and bitter within, which can then lead to ill health. She wants someone, especially her husband or partner, to notice what is happening to her but, wrapped up in his own life, he does not, for he just takes this as the norm for their family life. This is the way that it has always been as far as he can remember. Not only that, he has started to accept his wife or partner as the person that she has now become, to accept this as the norm for her. What both of them need is for her to love herself, for her to realise that all these good things are there for her too. The Universe is providing all this for her and, indeed, each surprise, each gift has her name on it and therefore she is not depriving anyone else, for they are hers. By going out and buying herself something from a state of self love she is acknowledging the fact that she, as well as her family, deserves to be happy, and deserves some of the luxuries that are being offered to her by the Universe.

By acknowledging that these are her entitlements she raises her own vibrations again. She radiates happiness, pleasure, laughter, self worth, self esteem and love – all very positive energies. And in radiating this energy her family see her in a different light. Her husband or partner sees her as the person with whom he fell in love. Her children see her as a beautiful individual who is also their mother and feel proud. Her parents remember her as the wonderful child with whom they were blessed. Her friends remember all the times that they have shared their problems with her and she has listened, and all the times of fun and pleasure that they have also shared. In enabling them to see her in this way she is enriching their lives. She is raising their vibrations. And therefore it is not a selfish act to look after and nurture oneself. Indeed it is a selfish act not to do this for oneself, for it has a detrimental effect on all those who come within your sphere.

By choosing to be a martyr, others feel drained in her presence and they feel guilty for buying things for themselves and they feel guilty for what they are receiving from her. Most of all they feel deprived of the beautiful being that they know instinctively they should have in their presence but who has chosen not to be with them except in this shadow form that she has created for herself. And so you see the martyrdom role that women so often take on is in nobody's best interests. So love yourself. Allow a little luxury back into your life and acknowledge how uplifting it is for you and consequently for all the others whose lives you touch.

The Boy King

The sky is red,
Red from the Sun's rays as it slips below the horizon.
The night animals commence calling to each other,
The owls begin to hoot, signalling their presence.
All over our hemisphere lights start to come on
In houses, offices, factories and streets.
People are coming home from work,
The children have returned from school,
A dog barks occasionally as it sniffs the air,
And then, lo, a brilliant white light appears in the sky.
It grows bigger and bigger until all that can be seen is light.
From the middle appears the most beautiful angel
Dressed in blue, with blue eyes to match.
He holds a child which we can all claim,
Saying "Never fear about this child, He is special,
He is in our care, we will look after Him."
So saying, a feeling of peace and contentment
Permeates the atmosphere.
People and creatures alike have a great sense of well-being,
For it is He, the Messiah, the boy king
Shown to us for our reassurance.
He is still there looking after us, sending us his unconditional love.
All we have to do is try to live as He did
And our future is assured.

Our World

How wonderful it is that nobody need wait a single moment
before starting to improve the world.

Anne Frank

*T*his beautiful Planet which we call home is full of negativity. We have deliberately chosen to be reincarnated here because of that very negativity. The challenge for us is to learn to become positive and to see all the wonderful things that there are in this world. For how can you become one thing if you have not experienced its absence? How do you know that you are happy if you have not been unhappy? How can you know the true beauty of something if you have not seen ugliness in its true form? Therefore it is by experiencing negativity that you realise you are given the choice to either remain in this state or to raise yourself and move into positivity. The real space to be in, ultimately, is one of perfect balance when negativity has been balanced by positivity and you can just be who you truly are.

When you raise your energy vibration from that of being negative you look at the whole world through different eyes. You see the same things but it is as though you are viewing it for the first time. You see beauty everywhere whereas before you had only seen ugliness. You meet people that you have had difficulty communicating with in the past but because you are looking at them with new eyes, you see their beauty, you see that which had previously eluded you. Therefore by changing your outlook you change your life. As more and more people do this, the energies on Earth will become less negative and less dense and the world will be seen as it really is. Do not worry if those around you cannot see what you can. It doesn't mean that you are wrong or that they are wrong, it just means that you are in a different space. We all walk our pathway at our own pace – sometimes walking, sometimes running and sometimes not moving at all!

The other day I was enthusing about the wonderful Sunset, the magic colours and how the sky was ablaze with these amazing pinks, reds and oranges. But no one else was excited. I wondered how they could all be sharing this moment of beauty with me but I was the only one who was appreciating it. Then it was pointed out to me that I should take off my sunglasses, which I did. No one else was wearing theirs and I could see why nobody thought the sky was beautiful because, without my sunglasses, there was no colour, just grey and white clouds. So you see, it didn't exist for them because they weren't coming from the same space as me. Although they were unable to see this, it didn't in any way lessen the beauty for me, because I could see it. When I put my sunglasses back on, I was able to see the final hues of what, for me, had been a spectacular Sunset. So, we were all correct: me for having seen the wonder of the Sunset, because I had, and the others because they had only seen a dull grey and white cloudy sky. It was just that we were in different spaces, we had different perspectives.

When you learn to love yourself you start recognising your interconnectedness with everything on Earth, and indeed in the Universe. You realise that the same spark of life, the same energy, that is in you is also in another person, a tree, a bird, an animal, an insect, a mountain, the sea and the Earth. In feeling this affinity, you know that you form part of the perfect chain of life and the love that you feel for yourself overflows into feeling love for all other living things. You realise that you could not do harm to any life form, because by harming them you are damaging yourself and you will also feel the pain.

Going shopping for food will take on a different meaning. If, for example, you buy a melon, you will marvel at its journey to reach you in order to give you nourishment and sustenance. The seed fell into the ground where it was incubated by the Earth, protected, kept warm and then brought to life by the rains. It forced itself into the daylight and grew, being fed by the goodness in the Earth, watered by the rains and nourished by the Sun. From that small seed grew a long trailing vine which, as it matured, produced fruit. All of this was provided by nature without any helping hand from mankind. The fruit was then picked, packed and transported to different countries around the world by a mixture of rail, road, air and sea, and eventually to the shop. The shopkeeper laid it out on display and you bought it. Think of the miracle of life's ability to create such goodness from itself to be able to sustain another form of life. This is the wonderful balance of our Universe whereby we have the Sun by day and the Moon and Stars by night. We have Mother Earth to nurture us and provide food for us and everything that we need for our comfort. It is important for us to appreciate what is provided by Mother Earth, not just for us humans, but for all the other inhabitants in our world.

Because there are fewer people now who grow their own food and have their own livestock, we tend to forget exactly how much time is put in by mankind and nature in creating this wonderful food for us which we need in order to live. We are also used to having our own car or using public transport and therefore rarely have much direct contact with the Earth and all its restorative energies. It is so important for us to walk regularly among natural areas like forests, beaches and mountains where everything is natural, unspoiled and unpolluted. We damage ourselves by continually living in areas that we have despoiled and that are created out of man-made material such as concrete. We forget who we are and what our natural heritage is. When we escape this false environment which we have made, we remember who and what we are. We are able to breathe more easily, we feel energised and we feel alive. We also remember how beautiful this globe is on which we live and vow to frequent the natural parts more often. In our day-to-day hygienic lives, where everything is disinfected and packaged for us, we are so distanced from what is really going on in the world that, unwittingly, we contribute to its destruction.

When we are greedy, we upset the balance and start raping what was given to us with love. We take, with no thought for the damage we are doing and the long-term consequences for the generations to come. We consider ourselves superior because of our brain, but it is dangerous to walk this pathway for, in adopting this attitude, we fail to learn the lessons that are there for the taking from everything that attempts to coexist with us.

Sometimes, in meditation, a wolf comes to me. He is strong, male, and powerful, and according to Medicine Cards by Jamie Sams and David Carson that I have, the wolf represents a teacher. He sets off on his own to have experiences and then he returns and teaches the others what he has learnt. In one particular meditation, he and I walked across the snow into a forest. It was night, the sky was clear with Stars shining, the Moon was full and bright and the branches of the trees were heavy with snow. Suddenly my spirit went into the wolf and I became one with him. My eyesight dimmed but my sense of smell was very strong. I then decided to see if I could move into one of the fir trees and join my spirit with its spirit the way I had with that of the wolf. I managed to do this and had fleeting impressions of the rain, wind, snow and Sun, animals climbing through my branches, and birds building their nests and rearing their young. It was all really beautiful. I also experienced a tree releasing its spirit when it was blown over in a storm, which was reassuring because it felt so natural and painless. I then returned into the wolf because I could see that he was sniffing something. It was a smaller animal and the wolf needed food for himself and his family. He asked the Universe for permission to kill this being. The little creature said it was time for his spirit to be released, so having received consent I, as the wolf, caught him, and just as the jaws shut on the little one's back, his spirit left. I, as the wolf, then carried the animal back to the cave where my mate and cubs were. It was a very profound meditation which showed me how all living things are linked.

Our forebears knew the importance of honouring all living things. They prayed before they planted their seed. This lifted the energetic vibration of the Earth where the seed was to be placed. Praying over their harvest as it grew again enhanced the energy of the growing plants. They prayed before they went on a hunt to the spirits of the animals they were going to kill for food and clothing. The animals were able to offer themselves willingly for they knew that their season on Earth had come to an end and they were prepared to sacrifice themselves for man. The meat was then prayed over before it was eaten, again raising the energies. They only ever took what they needed and left the land as they had found it for future generations to come and for all beings that shared the Earth with them; acknowledging themselves as caretakers, not owners.

In asking permission of the animal which you are about to kill, or asking permission of a tree to use it to build a house and receiving that permission, the energies are right for everything to be done the best way that it can be. The animal gives itself willingly and therefore there is no pain or anger in its energy. When the meat is prayed over, it raises the vibration so that in eating this meat, which goes directly into your body and becomes part of you, there is no pain, anger or lower energy for you to ingest. It is only the highest and best, giving you the finest nourishment both physically and energetically.

When you build your house from trees that have willingly given their life to provide shelter for you and you have prayed during the building and at the completion of your house, you are raising the energy levels. Therefore you are living continuously in a higher energy than you would have been if you had just taken the life of the trees without their consent. The pain that they would feel as you chopped them down when they died unwillingly would have become part of the fabric of your home and all the time that you were living in that house you would subconsciously be absorbing the pain which was being released. But by asking the tree and by blessing the building of the house, the energies are continually being raised and create a balanced harmonious home in which you and your family can live.

If there were problems between our forebears, they would start by praying and then both sides would speak their opinion. If they could not resolve their differences, they would sit prayerfully and wait until a solution arose from the inspiration of one who was present. They would then accept the solution and close the proceedings with another prayer. What they had done was open the meeting by energetically raising themselves and the meeting place. When they were unable to reach a solution using their mind, by raising their vibrations, and waiting in the silence, a solution was given to them from a higher source which satisfied the honour of both sides. If they had tried to limit finding the answer to a purely human level, it would have taken much longer and would not have been as balanced and as pleasing as the one that came from the higher source.

As with all great truths, this is simple but has become so complicated. The whole of life is the experience of giving and receiving between all life forms. The giving comes from the source of love and the receiving also comes from the same source. This, then, completes the circle whereby everything is balanced out perfectly. When this happens, all goes according to plan because everything is functioning on the higher vibrational levels, on the levels of positivity, not on the lower, denser levels of negativity. Greed is a negative energy. It is all about satisfaction for the one, regardless of the cost to everybody and everything else. Greed does not bring about fulfilment and peace of mind, unlike those who give and receive in love.

When you are in a space of self love, you want to live in peace and harmony with all things. It seems natural and right. You only want to use your energies for what gives you the best in life. Eating tainted food, whether it is animal, vegetable or mineral, is not in your highest interest. Living in a place where you feel uncomfortable and are unable to relax and feel at peace with yourself is not in your highest interest, and being in dispute with others is not in your highest interest. If, however, you recognise yourself as being part of every thing and every thing being part of you, you will only put out loving energies towards all; you will only want to see every thing being treated in the best possible way. You will want to raise the energies of your life in all things so that you can live as you are meant to live, on a higher plane and not where the denser energies are, among negativity. This will enable you to lead a happier, more positive and more loving life as you embrace yourself in whatever form you take. It will also open you up to the perfect flow of the Universe and bring you abundance that you had only ever dreamed about.

The Planet Earth, which you inhabit for such a short time in your present body, is a university of learning. It provides many opportunities for you to grow, to build your awareness of who you truly are and to be the beautiful energetic being that is you. All living things that you come across, and indeed there is very little on your Planet that is not living, are experiencing their own evolution process. In doing this, however slow and long the process may be, there are always changes. There are the rocks that crumble and join with the skeletons of small creatures to make the sand on the beaches. There is the drying up of some waterways, enabling you to walk along them, and there is the uninhibited gushing of the new spring as it surfaces and finds its own way down to the sea. There are the explosions of matter in the skies creating new Stars. There is the shifting of the plates on your Earth, changing the levels of the water, submerging some land and exposing other parts. All is change and all is to be respected.

Man considers that he is in control of all things at all times but it is part of his learning that there are indeed forces that are greater than him and that however well he thinks he has planned his human life, things can be changed in a fraction of a second. But for those who acknowledge that they are more than just human beings, there is the beauty and the wonder and the acknowledgement that all is right: everything has its place and its time. The more that you progress on your pathway energetically, the more you see the beauty of the world around you and the wonder of your own life, the magic moments that are given to you and the happiness that you encounter by truly aligning yourself with all life forms on your wondrous Planet.

Anger

Why am I so angry?
Why am I shaking like a volcano about to erupt?
Why am I so hot it feels as though my blood is boiling?
I thought I had dealt with all my issues,
All my anger had dissipated.
I was at peace with myself and the world.

I was content.

And now it feels as though I am only at the beginning,
My anger once ignited continues to well;
Why is this happening to me? I ask.

Then I see myself in sunglasses.
I realise that the outward show is hiding
Not only me from others, but me from myself.
I try to be everything that is expected of me,
A good daughter, mother, wife, friend, lover.

Be there for everyone – be a rock.

I needed space to find out who I really was
So I left my family and travelled across the world:
I did what no mother should – I abandoned my children.
I was desolate, I was lost.

Please tell me who I am.

I was not left on my own, however,
I was met and supported by wonderful friends.
There was no criticism and no judgement,
Just a cushion of love wherever I went
And then out of nowhere the anger began.

I seemed to have had so much to contend with
All through my life,
Why was I still living in such a turbulent state?
Then sudden realisation dawned.

Anger heralded my unresolved issues.

Without the anger I would not change.
Everything would be suppressed.
How could I change?
Why should I change
If I thought everything was fine?

I acknowledge now that there is still much to do
For I am more complex than I realised.
As each issue is resolved
It makes way for another.

Now I realise anger is my friend.

Whenever I feel it, the heat welling up,
I need to look to see what the cause is.
Then I look inward to see what to do
And deal with what upset me.

Each time I learn more of who I am.

So anger thank you for your help,
I know now that you were just masking my fear.
I am changing so fast,
I am growing so much,

I am recognising the truth of who I am.

Change

You must be the change you want to see in the world.

Mahatma Gandhi

*W*hy am I so frightened of change? Why do I oppose it so fiercely? Why do I dig my heels so firmly into the ground and have to be dragged along screaming? Why do I use my oars to stop myself going with the flow of the stream? Why do I make life so difficult and so tiring for myself? Why do I think that change will only bring bad things into my life? Why the fear?

It's true that we, as human beings, generally resist change because we are frightened of the unknown. Even if our present life is unhappy, it is one that we know and therefore there is a security in our unhappiness. We feel that stepping out of it could be worse than what we know already. For me, I always seem to have had to learn things the hard way because of my fear of change. I haven't been able to move forward by listening to other people's experiences. I have had to make my own 'mistakes' and have my own understanding, however painful that has been, whatever it has cost me, and however long and drawn out the lesson.

I feel as though I am trapped in this life, imprisoned against my will, locked up in jail with the key thrown away, stuck here forever. I have lost my independence, my freedom of spirit; I am tired, listless, and unable to think about challenges, let alone face them.

So what is it I really want? I want to stop feeling lonely. I want to feel loved. I want my family, including my parents, to be living in close proximity. I want to have the energy to face the day. I want to be happy. I want to know the direction I'm going in and follow it with a light but committed heart. I want to have friends. I want to have a purpose in life. I want to feel excitement. I want to have a good figure. I want to look great in my clothes and also in a bikini!

I am sitting in one of the most beautiful countries in the world, at my desk which faces the garden. At the moment it is summer, and so the ranch slider is open to let some breeze in as it is a very warm day. The sky is blue with a few white clouds adding interest. A plane flies by in the distance from Auckland airport. What an amazing invention. All those people, all that weight, carried safely around the world in a metal tube with wings. A dream turned into reality by man's mind. He is the creator of his own destiny. He can also be the undertaker. It depends whether he allows his mind to work for him by directing all that energy or whether he lets it take control of him and then create things for him that he doesn't need.

The cicadas are singing as a background choir while the birds perform their solos. The flowers in the garden are bright in their different colours despite enduring weeks of extreme heat. And if I sit up, I can see the harbour in the distance and the headlands that protect it from the sea. How can I fail to be happy? Why do I continue wanting to rush back to my old life? Is it the security of the familiar? But what guarantee do I have that I will be happy there anymore? Yes. I will be happy because of family and friends, rather like picking up your old teddy. It reminds you of secrets, comfort and familiarity. But you have to feel good inside because if you don't, wherever you are will not be enough to make you feel happy. The journey of life is not to go backward; it is to go ever forward, growing with knowledge and experience as you walk your pathway. Indeed, even if you try to go back to a situation from whence you have come, it will not be the same because you will already have changed. Not to acknowledge that to yourself means that you will not achieve the comfort and satisfaction that you thought you would feel by going back into a previous space in your life.

Change is good for you. Indeed it is essential in order for you to grow. One season flows into the next having prepared the way. Mankind follows the cycle of nature, as do all living things. Winter turns into spring followed by summer, autumn and then winter again. A natural circle of life. These seasons match our own life stages. Our gestation period is the same as the plants in the ground. Our birth and youth is as the spring, when lambs and the plants come back to life. We mature into the summer of our lives, move on to the experience, wisdom and reflection of the autumn, and return once more into the darkness of the winter in readiness to be born again.

If you are in one place and need to go to another you cannot miraculously just be there. You have to go on a journey to arrive at your destination and it is the former that is more important for you to experience than the latter, for it is the expedition that gives us the learning experience, not our predetermined place of arrival. There will always be the quick route where nothing is seen or learnt and you arrive at your destination no wiser, having blinkered yourself and been in too much of a rush to absorb or learn anything on the way (the low road). Or there is the journey that is challenging in every way, which tests you and brings out the best in you – that makes you grow (the high road). Both roads bring you to the same place, but by taking the high road you have changed and now have a different perspective on life. You have grown. You have moved on. You are able to understand other people's behaviours and viewpoints in a way you never could before. You have learnt. If, however, you take the low road you arrive at your destination exactly the same as when you set out, having learnt nothing and wondering why others have changed and progressed and you haven't.

All nature's changes of season, which we do not consider with trepidation, unlike our own natural transition (apart from those who favour one season more than another), are necessary for the next stage. The natural world instinctively goes through changes without the fear we know. She has the knowledge that, without alteration, nothing evolves, everything stands still, there is no growth. If there had been no transformation in our life, we would still be the egg waiting to be fertilised in the womb, or the baby unable to satisfy its own needs. Is this the way we would have it? No! So why do we get into such a panic about a natural progression.

Instead of feeling such fear about my new life, I could embrace it fully. I could be grateful to be experiencing such new opportunities that many do not have. I could feel great excitement about the new challenges which will face me today, knowing that I will learn from them however I address them. I could keep my eyes wide open for new openings which would not have come my way if I had not moved. I could find a purpose to my existence which is totally different from anything that I had imagined. I could go to bed at night and think back on the day, thrilled about all the new things that had come into my life. I can do all these things, if I don't allow fear to take hold of me; if I don't allow my mind to become negative as a result of the fear; if I don't lose control of my mind because of the negativity.

It is so easy – two scenarios; one choice. We should only ever regret the things that we don't do, not the things that we do. What I mean by that is, of course we sometimes regret the things that we have done. However, if we try something and it doesn't work out we have to ask ourselves why and see what lesson there is in it for us. Hopefully, if we are able to take on board our learning at that stage we will do things differently next time. And if we have done just that then there is no need for regret as we have learnt a valuable lesson and can look back at that situation with gratitude for what it has taught us. But if we never try something, we are always left wondering what would have happened and if it might not in some way have improved our life and assisted us on our journey of personal growth.

We are in control of our destiny. We are our own creator. We have a choice; we can see change as something to be fearful of and do our utmost to prevent it or we can welcome it with open arms seeing it as a wonderful chance to experience new things, learn more about ourselves and grow accordingly. It is far better to release the fear by stepping into it and seeing where your journey takes you. Unless you step out in a positive way, you do not know what wonderful opportunities are out there waiting to greet you. You can then move back into your old life, if that is your choice, but it will not be the same – it will be better. It will be enriched because you have grown by accepting and living the challenge.

So remember: everything is about you. Not someone else. YOU. You are in control of your life, you are not a victim and it is up to you how you meet the situations that arise on your pathway.

I am homesick but who does that benefit? Not the family I am with here, not the family I left overseas, and certainly not me. I don't want to spend all my time sad and with regrets about another wasted day. How much better for me and my loved ones if I create a new life for myself. How much more positive for those I live with and how much easier for those I am apart from if they can glean some solace from the fact that even though we are not together I am enjoying my new opportunities. Finally, but most importantly, how much more beneficial it is for me.

Here then are the two opposing sides of the mindset: negative feelings of unhappiness, helplessness creating weakness and a 'poor me' scenario; or positive feelings of achievement, growth, fulfilment and being in control of my own life. If I look at this from a point of loving myself there is only one choice, the choice which brings me nothing but positivity and whatever gifts and opportunities I receive as a result of this.

Change is a beautiful mother-of-pearl inlaid box which is presented to you. You hold the key in your hand and only you can decide whether you wish to unlock the box and open the lid, and see the secrets that are held inside. They are your secrets. They are for your eyes only. For only you can choose whether you wish to make these changes and grow, or whether you prefer to stay in the security of the life in which you find yourself in this moment in time. There is no wrong or right. There is only when you are ready.

When the time is appropriate for you, the secret that has been kept in the box will bring about such a welcome and exciting challenge for you. It will bring about such growth that with hindsight you will wish that you had taken this special offering from the box on an earlier occasion; but you must not have any self recrimination for the time is only right when it feels right for you. After all, this is your journey and no one else's. Enjoy the challenge of the change and the gifts that come with it.

The Marriage

As they stood there at the altar
The love they shared was true,
Each taking their vows
Meaning every word they said.

The years went by,
The vows were broken,
His love not being nurtured by hers
Returned as a seed to the ground.

It could not maintain its power,
Its beauty and its force
Without the loving gentle hand
Encouraging and responding.

For love flows.
For it to survive there must be a continuity
Of giving and receiving,
Of nurturing.

When it is only given by one
It slowly dries up,
All passion gone, all hope spent,
All communication lapsed.

But when shared by both
It grows, becoming ever bigger,
Changing to meet the wants and the needs.
Always there, giving support and understanding.

So marriage cannot survive
On the love of one alone.
However great that love,
Its needs must be reciprocated.

But love held the final key,
For when she told him she must go
He once again showed his love,
And despite his personal cost
He said goodbye with love.

It was in that moment
She realised what a great gift she had had.
How pure and beautiful his love
Which she had failed to nurture.

And now she sits on her own
Reflecting on her life,
She feels so honoured, so blessed
To have spent part with such a man.

'The jewel in her crown'
He had been called when they first wed,
An expression she couldn't understand
As she struggled through the days.

But today, finally she saw
A man of integrity, honesty and commitment,
A man of love and strength.
He had been her saviour.

All the lessons he had taught her
Had brought her to where she was today.
She had forgone most of her materialistic ways
Along with superficiality and lies.

He had brought her to a new land
Where she had been born again,
And now she had the strength to walk forward
With self love and no longer self hate.

This was thanks to him.
Even though his love was not nurtured
He gave her the greatest gift he could,
Her ability to finally love herself.

Self Love

To love oneself is the beginning of a lifelong romance.

Oscar Wilde

*S*o, it's time to love yourself. It's easy to say, but what exactly does it mean and how do you go about it? I was in a position of self hatred. I didn't like myself at all and nothing was going the way that I had planned it as a little girl. I put on weight which made me like myself even less because I didn't feel I looked attractive any more and I also considered that I looked like a lump of lard in my clothes! In reality, I had only put on one and a half stones but as I have a small frame with a height of 5'4", it certainly made all my existing clothes look tight-fitting. Because I was always intending to go on a diet, I couldn't see the point in buying new clothes which would have suited me better, and therefore for some considerable time I continued wearing clothes that were too close-fitting and were rapidly going out of date.

With the benefit of hindsight, I can see that it was because I did not love myself. I was most unhappy with the way that I was living and, therefore, felt that I did not deserve to be attractive or look good any longer. So, looking at myself in the mirror every day and knowing that I did not look good was my punishment, which subconsciously I thought I justly deserved. However, I blamed everyone else for my problems, not realising that I was the one who had actually created them. It was only when I started to read Louise Hay's book *You Can Heal Yourself* that I appreciated that I had to take responsibility for my life and the way it was. Initially, I was very sceptical and cautious, with my mind telling me, "Well, of course it was all right for her – she's different, but this is not true for you." But by being gentle with myself, I slowly began to realise that my mind could not always be relied on to tell me the truth. Up until that point, I had enjoyed what I considered, overall, to be a good relationship with my mind. It had helped me to become successful in my career and because it was able to look at issues from different angles it was a great help when I was negotiating, which was an important part of my job. My business life gave me a real buzz and I was secure in what I was doing.

My personal life, however, was somewhat different. As soon as emotions became involved my mind ceased to be my reliable friend and I would behave in a completely irrational way. However, as they say, what you need comes your way; but you have to be prepared to acknowledge its existence, be open to its suggestions and commit yourself to the pathway it shows. I had bought this book by Louise Hay many years ago and had read it with interest, but, at that stage, did not consider it to be particularly relevant to me. However, this time it was different. I came across the book unexpectedly, having forgotten that I had it, and started reading. Your mind is similar to a computer and is programmed by your experiences, both in this life and your former lives, and in your genetic makeup. It also enjoys having control over you. It has heard you express negative remarks about yourself repeatedly and so this is what it continually replays to you. It sees that what it is doing is protecting you even though this attitude is seriously misguided. It is never too late, however, to retrain your mind. The saying that 'you can't teach an old dog new tricks' does not apply in this instance, whatever your age!

The first thing for you to do is to look at yourself as you would your best friend, for in reality this is what you should be, and accept who you are with deep love and understanding. After all, you know the difficulties, the sadness and grief that have crossed your path and only you know how you have reacted to every situation at the time that it happened. Do not beat yourself up about anything that you have done because this will not help you to change. It doesn't matter what you have done in your past because it is the present that is important, and it is the present that creates the future, just as it was your past which has created the now. So look at yourself with loving eyes, with eyes of concern and sympathy. Know that all your past experiences have brought you to this very place. There have been no successes or failures, there has only been learning. Loving yourself is all about being and looking the best you can because you love yourself so much that you don't want to be any less than you can be.

A major issue these days is your physical shape and size. In some cultures it is important to be large as it shows that you are wealthy and have plenty of food to eat, while if you are poor you are skinny because you cannot get enough food and also have to work very hard. However, in the Western culture, overweight people are considered unattractive because our magazines are full of pictures portraying slim models and therefore subliminally stating that only slim is beautiful. It doesn't matter, however, whether you are skinny or overweight if the outer covering fails to show the magnificence and the true beauty of who that person really is within, and for those who take the trouble to look at themselves and others they will find the truth of who that soul is. Within reason it is fine to be large or to be skinny but it has to be balanced against health issues, and wherever there are extremes then it means that there is a lack of self love.

Very slim girls have an incorrect mental image of themselves and see themselves as fat and ugly, and overweight people are very often unhappy and comfort-eat. Some of our eating habits are because of the way we have been brought up and the circumstances around those and other habits are because of our feelings of insecurity and lack of self worth. However, there are many serious issues around food – whether you are eating too much or not enough, whether you are anorexic or bulimic, it is important that your issues are addressed as speedily as possible because in all instances it amounts to an abuse of body and of self. As our body is our home while we are in human form and living on Earth, if we destroy it we destroy our home and can no longer live on this Planet. So whether you are someone who has weight issues or you are someone looking in from the outside, it is so important that you learn and recognise the truth of who you/they are, work through the issues that surround this and learn to love yourself.

Your size doesn't dictate who you are – it's what's inside you – your soul and your heart, and they know who you really are, so allow that knowledge to radiate through because the truth of you is far more beautiful and permanent than any body shape. When you hear about the journeys that people who have had weight issues have taken, which have sometimes gone on for very many months or even years, you are told that they all have a much higher opinion of themselves now. They are thrilled with how they look, the energy they have and the improvement of their health and life within their family and relationships. Their starting point was their soul, deep inside them, managing to inspire them to start walking on this pathway of self love.

As a child, if you touched something hot, you didn't do it again because it hurt. But you didn't consider that experience to be a failure. It was, indeed, even a success because you have learnt from it. Imagine what would have happened in your life if after your first attempt to walk you gave up because you hadn't succeeded, you'd fallen over. But you didn't give up, did you? You kept on trying until you mastered it. It is important that you remember this in your daily life. Keep trying until you achieve what you want. Each experience you have has given you the opportunity to learn and has therefore been successful. If you did not want to change things, then you would not have picked up my book. The reason that you have done this is because you know that now is the time to improve the quality of your life and you are hoping that this book is your signpost pointing to a happier and more fulfilling pathway.

To retrain the mind and replace the negative statements and thoughts that you have carried around with positive statements, you need to repeat the positive statements over and over again. This is exactly what you have done with the negative comments over the years. In this way, your positive statements will supersede the negative ones. Every time you find yourself starting to say "I can't" or "I won't" or any other negative expression, change it immediately to "I can" and "I will" and eventually you will find that you are saying these words automatically.

The most important affirmation to say is "I love you" or "I love myself," whichever feels more comfortable to you. Initially, look at yourself in the mirror when you say this. Look deep into your eyes. Don't worry, if to begin with, you don't feel any emotion as you say these words, in fact your initial reaction will probably be one of embarrassment and a great wish to laugh, as well as to make sure that no one in the house can hear what you're saying!

I know mine was. But gradually you will come to realise that, the more you say it, the more you start to feel a surge of love, a warmth welling up inside you towards yourself. You need to say these words over and over again while looking in the mirror, taking a shower, having a walk, driving somewhere, even going to the toilet! Just keep chanting these words continuously because, remember, you are replacing the countless times in your life that you have made a negative statement about yourself. Can you estimate how many times you have done this? – because that will give you a good idea of how many times you now have to say you love yourself. Trust me, stick with it. I didn't feel anything for quite some time, because I had regularly beaten myself up over the years, but I was determined not to give up and eventually I started to feel love for myself. It is at this point that you start to change your life.

You realise that most of what you do in your life, or maybe even everything you do, is done for other people. This is not always in your best interests. Having recognised this, you can now start to make changes. Stop trying to be the perfect wife/husband, mother/father, sibling, friend etc rushing around everywhere, trying to please everyone else. All that happens is that you end up by being frustrated and bad-tempered because you have not done what you want to do for yourself. Start by questioning each action before you do it: "Is it in my highest and best interest to do this?" "Because I really love myself is this the right thing for me to do at this time?" and listen to the answer. You will feel great relief when you know the truth.

Having ascertained what the truth is for you in this situation, implement it in a loving way. You'll be pleasantly surprised at the reactions of the other people, for the truth isn't just right for you, it is right for everyone else too. It invites, indeed encourages, new learning for all those around you. It stops them from being selfish and allows them to consider others. It prevents you from being the martyr and enables you to be a real person. It addresses the issue of you being exhausted and snappy. Truth enables you to live your life the way that it is meant to be lived rather than just existing. It also means that when you do something for someone else, you do it willingly and with love. They will appreciate it far more than when you do it because you have to and therefore do it grumpily. It puts you in the right space to make the best decisions for yourself. Otherwise, you can make a choice which you later regret because you were in the wrong space at the time.

Loving yourself and, as a result, living your truth, is important for everyone. Imagine the quantity of negativity which is daily being put into our world. Consider the amount of negative things that you say and think during the day, multiplied by all the other people who are struggling with their lives like you. How much better it is to wake up and feel excited about the new day. Regard each day as a blank page where anything could happen, an exciting opportunity could arise, a positive thought you had could materialise.

You can write your own affirmations about any area of your life which you wish to improve. One of my favourites is "Today is one of the best days of my life." I have used this where something has happened to upset me and I have gone to the cloakroom, wiped away my tears, looked at myself in the mirror and repeated this over and over again, as well as "I love myself" of course, until I have felt strong enough to go back out. On every occasion that I have said this, the situation that has upset me has changed at some stage during the day, sometimes even instantly, or something completely unexpected has happened, and I have indeed ended up having one of the best days of my life. When I am going out in the car, before I leave my home, I think positively about getting a parking space and visualise approximately where it will be. I always get one. My friend, however, who tells me that she can never find a car parking space, never does. So what does that say about the power of positive and negative thoughts?

Another friend of mine started a new job. Everyone she worked with was telling her how brilliant she was at it and she felt great. Then, for no apparent reason, they started criticising her, which caused her to experience a real emotional dip and feel she wasn't any good at what she was doing. The lesson here, for her, was to learn that she didn't love herself enough. While she was being praised she was living off the energies of everyone's adulation, so, similarly, when the rejection came she absorbed their negative energies as well. The awareness this brought to her was that she has to love herself totally, and also to connect to the Universe for her energies, because then they will always be there for her, rather than to other human beings because they are not always consistent.

Loving ourselves is as important to us as breathing, because in loving ourselves not only does our life change for the better but, because we come to realise what a struggle we have had, we can look at others with the knowledge that within them is also a centre of love that they have clouded by being negative about themselves. We therefore see them in a different way and feel love for them, because an angry, aggressive person is a person who is hurting and unhappy inside. If they weren't feeling like that, they would not be behaving in this way. Therefore, to react to their anger in a similar manner only fuels their fury, but being calm and loving towards them diffuses the situation and indeed touches their centre of love, however well hidden it is. In the first instance, your negativity adds to the negativity which they are already experiencing, but in the second instance your positivity finds a chink in the negativity and helps to reduce the negative energy around that person. So you can see how important it is to turn all your negative thoughts about yourself to thoughts of love and also all your negative thoughts towards others and towards negative situations into positive ones.

There is a divine plan of which we are all part, but our human intelligence is too limited to understand this. I know that when I love myself and walk in truth and trust, everything that I need in my life comes to me provided that I am open to all the opportunities that come my way.

If you consider that every thought that you have, and every word you speak, creates your future, that every now becomes your future, you will see how important it is to only have the right thoughts and speak the correct words. It is your choice. You can create a positive future or a negative one. The reason that we are on Earth is to learn, and to resolve all our different issues over a period of lifetimes. I would liken us to an onion. A situation presents itself to us and when we have dealt with this situation, a layer is peeled away. In doing this, we expose a new layer with new issues and new challenges for us. These could not have been dealt with or addressed prior to the first layer being peeled away, and so it continues. But the more aware you are of this process taking place, and the more that you love yourself, the more you become attuned and so the quicker you resolve these matters. I have had many issues that have lasted for years, such as suffering low self esteem, not feeling deserving and not honouring myself. I've put everyone's needs before mine and worn myself out. I have kept going round in circles wondering what the problem was, but since I have learnt to love myself everything has become easier and more straightforward. Now, I face my challenges knowing that I will grow from my learning as opposed to ignoring them or hiding from them in fear.

In loving yourself, you begin to know yourself and what you really need, not what you think – or have been told – you need.

Self love connects you to the Universe. Trust in what is happening in your life. Go with the flow. Leave your comfort zone and grow as a result of this. You will walk a different pathway because of the way in which you look at yourself and, because of the change in you, others will want to know what has happened. You will find that you are, indeed, leading by example.

Self love is the greatest gift that you can give to yourself. In loving yourself, you will only attract the highest and the best. Self love is accepting who you truly are, a being of light, a child of the Universe. It will enable you to walk where you had only dreamed of walking before. It will enable your wishes to come to fruition in the right way for you. It will create happiness and balance in your life.

Every time you are given a challenge, start by remembering how much you love yourself and the outcome will be different than if you were coming from a place where you did not love yourself. Every time you tell yourself that you love yourself you raise your energies and vibrations and therefore attract only those higher energies and vibrations than otherwise you would have done. So, my child, for the sake of your learning and evolution, ensure that each day, you are fully aware of how much and how important it is to love yourself.

Growth Follows Pain

My heart is torn and bleeding
Tears course down my face
My body is battered, bruised and pummelled
I am lost, sinking without a trace
My mind in trying to protect me
States that he is to blame
But my soul begs me to listen to my pain.

There is a lesson there for me
Right within the core of this hurt
And when I go there and listen
Gradually I will become complete.

But was it really his fault
Or was I in the wrong?
Is it ever just one person
Or do we both contribute?

We chose to be together
Because of the love we felt
But neither of us was free from baggage
Our past, our issues came too.

Do I look at us as just a destructive time
Or do I choose to see the part we both played
With all our different facets chinking together?
How much better if out of all this hurt
Something good could be born.

If I can forgive both you and me
Address my problems, move on
Knowing that out of pain comes growth
Out of dark comes light
Then am I reborn happier, more content
Less baggage, fewer issues and my story continues.

I can move forward to the next page
As I continue walking my life's pathway.

I Want / I Need

I may not have gone where I intended to go,
but I think I have ended up where I needed to be.

Douglas Adams

*W*ith self love comes a change in how you view your life. Why are you spending your time working so hard? What are you hoping to achieve? Why don't you have enough free time to do what you want for yourself? Why don't you see as much of your family as you want? Why don't you see your friends so often? Why are you so tired? What happened to the quality of your life? Why do you need a new house/car/holiday? Is it because you truly need it or is it just on your want list because of media pressure, so you can keep up with your friends, make your partner happy or give yourself a quick fix, or do you feel it is expected of you so you can show everyone how well you are doing and how successful you are?

We live in a very materialistic age and the pressures that are on us to keep up with everyone else and with technology are onerous. We turn on the television, and there is someone trying to convince us that we can't live without the latest gadget. We turn on the radio, and our ears are bombarded with advertisements telling us that this product is the answer to all our difficulties and that we must buy it. Then there are all the advertising hoardings lining the streets. Our children badger us about what their friends have and how they must have the same. And at Christmas time it all intensifies to such an extent that you feel a failure if you are unable to buy your husband, wife, partner, boyfriend, girlfriend, parents, grandchildren, grandparents, children and friends what they so richly deserve! Instead of having an enjoyable time with friends and family and remembering that Christmas is a religious festival, you are so stressed out you don't enjoy it. No wonder so many relationships break up at Christmas.

All this pressure is having a negative influence on us and in order not to lose face and deprive our children we either make ourselves ill by working every available hour to earn the money that we need, spend money that we do not have by using our credit cards or buy items on hire purchase. It all sounds so easy at the time: "Buy this suite now and you don't have to pay anything for six months." Yes, fine. But what if you still don't have the money in six months' time, what if you've lost your job, what if you become sick, what if you and your partner separate, what if someone dies, and so the list goes on. It's the same with the credit cards. Just pay a little off each month, they say. Great. But the interest rate is so high that if you owe a large sum of money your payments may only be keeping pace with the monthly interest you are incurring. And even worse – if you are unable to pay all the interest off every month, then you will be charged interest on the outstanding interest as well. So the vicious circle continues and you become more and more depressed about it, to the extent that it affects your every waking hour. You no longer want to emerge from the covers of your bed because you don't feel you can face the day ahead, let alone the world any more. There is no joy or pleasure in your life.

There are some who refuse to even acknowledge the problem until their whole world crashes around their ears. Even if you do manage to just about keep up with the payments – guess what? It's little Joey's birthday, it's your Mum's birthday, it's a friend's silver wedding anniversary, there's a school trip and, "Oh No it's Christmas again!" Your life is in such a precarious state. You are so unhappy that you are shouting at your loved ones and the atmosphere around you is terrible for all concerned. OK, so you got yourself into this state and situation because you thought it was the right thing to do. But how can it be when it has brought you such despair?

Now consider the other scenario, the one of loving yourself so much that you are not going to allow yourself to get into a financial mess. So you wanted a new car because your friends have just had new ones. If they are real friends they won't think any less of you because you still have your old but faithful car. After all, it's your company that they value, isn't it? It's who you are that matters to them, not what you own. Your kitchen needs modernising but it's still serviceable. So keep using it. You can put some money on one side to save for a new one if it's really important to you. The settee is old but you can still get some more wear out of it. The children can have inexpensive Christmas presents and learn the value of what they are given with a loving heart. My children used to make me things as my Christmas presents and I have valued these more than those that they have bought for me. Of course, the true benefit to your offspring is that they won't end up with a suicidal parent. How often has a child seen something on the television, wanted it desperately, been given it for Christmas and then, after a few days, never played with it or used it again and it gets pushed to the back of the cupboard to gather dust?

You see, we have to make the right decision for ourselves, the decision that brings us the greatest peace, the decision we make because we love ourselves. This is our choice. Having made our decision and spoken this truth lovingly to those whom it concerns, their reaction is their issue and their challenge. It is for them to deal with accordingly. Because when you come from a point of inner truth, it is always right for everyone, even if it may not seem that way at the time. It is not for you to protect them from what they need to learn by not living your truth. I know that you do it with the best intentions in mind but how do you know what they need to learn in order to grow? So whether it is family, friends or strangers, the best gift that you can give to them is that of living and speaking your truth with love, because not only will that put you in the right space to be in, it will also put them in the right space.

It is so important for us human beings to walk the pathway of self love and truth and not bow down to any outside pressure. You will also find that this will help to make you a more balanced person who can live happily despite lacking the material possessions we tell ourselves we cannot live without. There are many people who do not know inner happiness and achieve excitement and fulfilment by going out and buying something new. But this fulfilment is only temporary because it is a quick fix for what is missing in their life – their love for themselves, their inner peace. And when they die they have to leave all their material possessions behind. They leave this life without having evolved in the way that they had hoped they would before they were reincarnated. As the Bible states, "It is easier for a camel to go through the eye of a needle than for a rich man to enter the Kingdom of God," because they have cushioned themselves from the world with their material possessions instead of going deep into themselves and growing as a soul.

So next time you want something and you can't really afford it, ask yourself whether you really need it. Most of the time, you'll find that you don't, and by making the decision not to have it you are preventing your truth from becoming distorted. If there are many things that you need but you can't afford them all, prioritise and buy those at the top of the list, then hold back until you can afford the others. When you have to wait and save for something, you often find it has more value when you are finally able to go out and buy it. It becomes more precious. Items which you just go and buy are not so special because there has not been the anticipation. All it cost was money – you have actually not contributed anything to the experience of the purchase.

I have a very dear friend whose husband has an extremely successful business career. She can afford to go out and buy anything she wants but this does not afford her the pleasure and excitement that she used to get in the days when they were struggling financially and she had to save up for what she wanted. So those of us who are not wealthy may envy the rich and think, "If only I had money my life would be perfect." It wouldn't! Because it isn't the money that makes your life perfect, it is you living your life to the full by loving yourself, being honest and truthful to yourself and everyone in your life, being balanced and being mindful of all opportunities which come your way because you have attracted them.

Many years ago, I desperately needed a new pair of shoes but couldn't afford to buy any. I had to visit a friend in London and as we were walking along one of the back streets we found a shoe shop. There in the window was a pair of shoes which were just the style I was looking for. Even better they were in the sale, and on offer at a very low price which I could afford. I went into the shop and, yes you've guessed it, they fitted me perfectly. So I had my pair of shoes. I find that this is what the Universe does for me all the time. I, consciously or subconsciously, send out a thought for something I want and I get it. Sometimes it's almost instant, at other times it takes years, depending on what it is I want and how urgently the Universe thinks I need it.

I have always wanted to travel extensively and regretted the fact that I did not have the opportunity after I left school or after I had finished my training. Years rolled by, I married and we had family holidays, sometimes abroad and sometimes at home in Britain. My husband had been in the Navy and I envied the countries that he had visited and his experiences. So when he suggested we move to New Zealand for a few years as an adventure I decided it would be an exciting thing to do. Travelling around New Zealand was amazing – it is such a beautiful country with so many natural wonders – but the UK, where my friends and family were, was too far away. I had to make regular trips between the two countries for family reasons, complaining about the distance and wishing we had gone somewhere nearer, such as France – one and a half hours' flight to Birmingham instead of at least 27 from New Zealand to London.

While I was moaning about this one day, I had a sudden realisation. This was what I'd asked for on many occasions over the years – the opportunity to travel – and now here it was. I'd been given it and instead of appreciating it for what it was, all I was doing was being belligerent. These trips half way across the Planet, sometimes flying east, sometimes flying west, were giving me the opportunity to see countries I'd only ever dreamed about. When I realised that this was my wish that had been granted, my perspective altered totally. I went from negative into positive mode, stopped moaning and realised how lucky I was. The same situation, but seen through different eyes, turned my experiences from a nightmare into a dream come true. As a friend of mine is fond of saying, "Be careful what you wish for, it may come true." I would like to add to that: "Make sure you recognise that your wish has been granted and enjoy!"

In relationships, need is a different matter. It is wonderful to be really needed by someone, to be told how much your opinion matters and to be consulted about everything before any decision is made. It makes you feel so important, it gives you the confidence in yourself you didn't have before, it gives you security and a feeling of belonging, no longer being lonely and bobbing around on the sea of life like a piece of flotsam. The reason you are feeling so good is because of the highly charged energies which the other person is projecting on to you. You are absorbing them and feeling as high as a kite! However, after a bit, their neediness starts to feel similar to a millstone around your neck. Their need is so great that they continually want to know where you are, what you are doing. The curse of the mobile phone emerges – they can ring you at any time. They start using their need as a controlling device. You begin to realise that their need is draining you and that you are feeling like a prisoner. You no longer do what you would normally be doing because you are too tired and, anyway, they might need you. Eventually, you rebel for the sake of your survival and grab your freedom back with both hands.

Let's look at the dynamics of such relationships in a little more detail. The person who is the needy one feels that they cannot travel through life on their own. They need someone to always be there, continually support them and give them the energy they need. Although flattering initially, no one is strong enough to carry someone else's weight throughout their life. When viewed from the point of self love, not only is it not in their highest and best interest but it is not in the highest and best interest of the needy person, either. The relationship ends and the needy person is left feeling even more insecure and needy than before, going through life accumulating more and more emotional baggage until ultimately they learn the lessons the Universe is giving them and analyse themselves through the eyes of self love realising that they have the strength they need within them.

In a relationship where each party needs the other, initially it is a strengthening time for each person due to the high level of energy which they are sending to each other. When the balance starts changing and outside factors intrude into the relationship, such as careers, children, elderly parents, even friends, the one who is no longer the focus of the need feels disorientated, dispirited and doesn't quite know where they fit into the relationship any longer. The secret here, and indeed in the previous case, is not to need anyone. Need is not necessary for a full, healthy, happy and balanced relationship; it could even be damaging. The need to be needed arises because we feel insecure about ourselves and another person's need makes us feel secure. The problem with this is that we are relying on someone else for our safekeeping and at any time this could change. When this happens, it leaves us in a state and feeling insecure again, only more so this time.

In summary, need is unhealthy when a person is having a relationship with someone else to feel secure and be the focus of attention – to feel needed. This can only be a temporary state of affairs, as ultimately it is too draining for the other person to continue this relationship, leaving the needy person feeling even worse than before the relationship began.

However, need is healthy when being in a state of self love in a relationship, as it instigates speaking your truth in order to change a situation that is not in your best interest. Also, by honouring your needs, such as going on holiday, going on a course or having an experience you will bring yourself fulfilment. This may or may not include your spouse or partner, again based on your best interests, but it all contributes to and improves your relationship that is being shared on a balanced and equal footing; remembering that what is in your best interest is also in the best interest of your partner.

A good relationship is about loving another person and wanting the best for them, but a totally successful relationship can only be achieved when each person is completely secure within themselves and living their life in complete truth. If you are absolutely secure in yourself then you will always feel this – it cannot be taken away by anyone else. And we achieve this inner security by self love. There may be times in our learning and our life's experiences when we feel threatened but, by remembering how much we love ourselves, we will quickly resolve any doubts, recognise what we are being faced with and regain our equilibrium.

'Want' and 'can't' are negative words. 'Choosing' and 'needing' are the positive words. Speaking your truth makes you strong, whereas negativity makes you weak: it appears to be strong but when challenged with the strength of truth, it crumbles. Because every word has its own vibrational energy, as you speak it, you can actually feel the vibration affect your being and the empowerment it brings when the word is spoken on a higher energy level. It makes you feel wonderful and capable of walking forward in your truth and able to confront anything. You feel so empowered that it seems as though you are embracing the whole world, as though you are at the head of an enlightened army. You are truth and are leading the army of love, light, joy, happiness and peace. This is your battalion. With you as truth, and this battalion behind, you have a deep knowing that you can confront any negative issues, such as hatred or anger.

I know that when I need something, it is right for me to speak the words to the person concerned. It is recognition of what I need to complete me as a human being, to contribute to my self love, as to who I am. This is not a want, it is a need, and by speaking it, the situation will change because of the vibrational energies of truth that are being used, altering the energetic levels around me.

"I want" says the child, because he wants attention but needs love. "I want" says the adult, because he wants attention but needs love. This is the story of the human life. He realised when he was quite small that in demanding something, he will get attention, whether it is the loving attention which is what he really needs, or whether it is attention where someone is shouting at

him. He considers that being shouted at is better than receiving no attention at all. And so the child grows into the adult with the same mindset, demanding things of himself and of others, when what he really needs is love. He looks to others to give him the love that is necessary to enhance his life. When this is not always forthcoming, his wants grow, his demands become bigger. When, however, he addresses his real need, the emptiness within, he realises that by connecting himself with the Universe, by giving himself the love that he craves, he no longer has to say that he wants, as he is being blessed with everything that he needs.

Self Esteem

Why should I be hurt by what you say?
Because it affects my self esteem.
Why does it matter to me what you say?
Because it affects my self esteem.
WHY?
I should not rely on the outer world for this,
I have everything I need internally.

I am unique.
I am of the Light.
I am an important link in the chain.
I am part of everything and everyone.

If I rely on the world to make me feel complete
I will always be disappointed.
But, if I go internally, then there is the truth,
The beauty of who I really am.
And in seeing and remembering,
I know I can walk with confidence and love,
Self love and self esteem.

Accountability

But penance need not be paid in suffering ... It can be paid in forward motion. Correcting the mistake is a positive move, a nurturing move.

Barbara Hall

*W*e are all accountable for every action we take, every thought we have and every word that we speak. However much we try to deny this, ultimately, we have to face what we have done, thought or said. If we are lucky, it will be in this lifetime, if not then it will be in a future life.

Fear of the outcome once we admit what we have done often holds us back from speaking the truth, but the longer we delay, the worse the situation becomes. If we accept that we are responsible for everything that happens to us, this is very empowering. It puts us in control of our own life, we are in the driving seat, we are no one's victim and if we are able to love ourselves then this becomes a daily reality for us. We realise that everything that happens to us was created for a learning process and, instead of feeling fear, we should embrace the situation, deal with it and then see what we have learnt as a result, remembering that there is no such thing as failure. Do not be angry with yourself over past decisions that you have made, as there is no such thing as a wrong decision and they have made you who you are today.

Many situations arise where we cannot escape our accountability. For instance, women cannot deny having shared an intimate moment with a man when they give birth nine months later, although the man can. We cannot deny having our tongue pierced because others can see the stud, or if it is not there, the hole. We cannot deny being in a fight if there is a black eye to prove it. These are all occasions where we are forced to face up to our actions because, visually, there can be no denial. Because we are accountable, the events are out in the open and the outcome can be dealt with, leaving us free to move on.

If it is a non-visible situation, you may choose to remain silent because you are not being forced into being accountable for your actions. This may seem like the ideal solution at the time but, it is the most destructive one for you. If you look at this decision from a point of self love, you will see that the only choice you can make is to tell the truth. Be accountable for whatever it is that you have done, do whatever you can to set it right and learn from the whole experience. This will set you free. If you are functioning from a lack of self love then the decisions you make will be negative ones. You allow your mind to dictate to you and not your heart. You will hear all the reasons why you shouldn't be accountable – because you'll get into trouble, because your friends won't like you, because you'll no longer be allowed to be a member of the gang, because…, because…, and so you keep silent. But the knowledge that you have not spoken out, however deeply suppressed, will not go away and it will build and build inside you, ultimately causing you problems, until you finally resolve it by speaking your truth. It is never too late.

By allowing your mind to convince you to go down the negative pathway of fear, you are being judgemental of how everyone will react to you if you hold yourself accountable. You are slipping more into the darkness which is caused by the absence of light. But this is not just about being accountable to others – it is about being accountable to you. You deserve the best out of life; you deserve happiness, joy and abundance. How can you get this if you are not living in accordance with your higher knowledge, in awareness of loving yourself and speaking your truth? By being accountable, you will experience a wonderful feeling of relief as you speak out and do whatever you must do to atone for your actions. Once it is out in the open, it is dealt with, it is cleared. It is no longer your guilty secret that lurks in the dark recesses of your mind, hovering there and waiting for the ultimate day when someone tackles you about it or makes some sly remark. Because, make no mistake, what goes around comes around and however well hidden your secret is, it will always come back to haunt you at some stage in your future.

Accountability does not have to be about a large issue. It relates to all things in your life, however trivial, on a daily basis. The more you accept accountability and realise your personal responsibility for everything you do, the more empowered you become. This makes you more aware of who you are, what feels comfortable for you and what actions ensure you feel content and at peace with yourself. Then the choices that you make will be different from those that you made before, when you were not feeling any love for yourself. You also realise that you are enjoying your life more fully and are able to make decisions that are more appropriate for the person you are. By doing this you will still, of course, be accountable for everything that you do, but you will be doing it from a point of light and positivity as opposed to dark and negativity.

I was procrastinating this morning, deliberately finding all sorts of important things to do instead of sitting down and writing this chapter. As I hadn't written anything for a few days, I was feeling a sense of anxiety inside me, a churning, a fear, and so I kept delaying facing these emotions. Finally, I knew that things wouldn't improve until I faced my issue. As I sat and meditated, I realised that I had created the circumstances to enable me to write this book, which was what I wanted to do. Therefore, I should be feeling excited about having such a wonderful opportunity instead of being anxious. The realisation came – I had to be accountable to myself for what I had created, and by being accountable I needed to honour my creation and enjoy it. As always, whenever I have a realisation, I instantly felt so much better and definitely uplifted. I realised that my creation is an extension of myself and therefore must be loved accordingly. Then, looking at it objectively, but with love, I can decide whether I am happy with this creation or whether I want to change it. Is it bringing me happiness or is it bringing me pain? If it's bringing me pain, why? What do I need to do to address the pain and allow it to dissolve? In my case it was a question of wanting my creation to continue, but needing to dissolve the fear so that I could enjoy what I had.

Emotions are always an important trigger for what we need to learn. So when we make ourselves accountable, it gives us the opportunity to see what emotional reaction we get. We can then explore these emotions and assess the feedback. We can, then, gently and with great self love, work on them and feel them dissolve.

A person who denies their accountability lives by a different set of rules from the person who is accountable. Gary Zukav, in his book *The Seat of the Soul* states that "evil is the absence of light." What a simple statement, but how powerful and, when realised, how obvious. The soul that is trapped in its own darkness can only see and do negative things. It continually does bad things because it has no light to help it change. A person who is evil does indeed deserve to be held accountable by the society where he lives and be punished accordingly. However, it is so important that any action taken towards him comes from the light, the positive energy of compassion as opposed to the dark, the negative energy of anger and vindictiveness. If all you do is send him more negative energy, you are not only not helping this soul in distress, but you are also damaging yourself by emulating him – he has no compassion and neither do you. So you are allowing darkness to come into your soul, which is bringing misery and negativity with it. By feeling compassion for this soul, which has put itself into a completely dark and evil situation, you are sending it light that will pierce the darkness and start helping it consider how it can amend who it is.

Imagine: the richer you become in self love, the more you are able to give real love from your heart and soul and the more you can radiate light on every level. Continuing this idea – if this is happening all over the world, you can see, in your mind's eye, how the light is growing and getting ever stronger. You can visualise people working on the dark, negative emotions they hold within them. Replacing these with light and love, they glow ever brighter, and the sheer force of this brilliance touches all the souls who know nothing but evil and darkness, piercing their depths and ultimately helping them to become light beings. What a wonderful vision. But it is happening, as more and more people become aware of their accountability to themselves to be who they really are, living their own truth in love instead of living how others have told them to be.

My daughter had her 16th birthday party at home. She invited about 50 friends initially, but somehow the number grew to 100 before her big night. She knew everyone who was coming so there were no gatecrashers, which was my main concern. At the end of the evening, when nearly everyone had gone, it came to light that some money, digital cameras and mobile phones had gone missing. The owners were all understandably upset and my daughter was so hurt that one of her trusted friends, whom she had invited into our home, could behave in such a way – abusing her hospitality and stealing from people who were the culprit's schoolmates.

The following day, the identity of the thief came to light and eventually the cameras were returned. It was decided that we should report the matter to the police because it was a crime and the phones and money were still missing. The culprit denied that he had taken the money or the phones. There were many issues here and my daughter and her friends, through the course of the next few days, worked their way through them. First there was anger, hurt and the coming to terms with the loss of what was theirs and what that loss meant to them. Then there was the experience of deciding to report it to the police because an offence had been committed and, finally, actually going to the police station.

They spoke to a helpful and supportive constable, which hopefully would make them feel comfortable speaking to the police again if they should ever need to in the future. There was hope that the police might be able to recover their belongings. There was disappointment when only some of their items were returned, and their anger at school when their schoolmate culprit seemed to have difficulty understanding what he had done wrong.

But as well as being really angry with him, they also experienced compassion for him. They kept thinking of things that had happened to him in his life and, whereas they didn't condone his actions, they started to understand why he might have done these things. There was also the hope that their going to the police would make him accountable and that he might learn from the experience and not repeat this, or commit an even worse crime. I was most encouraged to hear these young people work through their negative emotions and come to such a positive conclusion. I hope this shows us the world's future. It also pleased me to see how important they thought it was to be accountable for your actions. They are so right.

Ensure that, above all things, you are always accountable to yourself. Question the emotions, reactions and thoughts that arise as a result of any action taken by you with love and learn from the answers. By doing this, you will notice a shift in awareness, creating a change in your behaviour which will make it easier for you to walk the pathway you have chosen for this lifetime.

In your materialistic world everything has its price. You go to the shop to buy some milk and at the till you have to account for what you have bought to the shopkeeper, and he has to account for the price to you. Items then exchange hands, whether it be money or some other commodity that the shopkeeper is prepared to take, and then you are free to walk out with what you have bought because, by being accountable for what you want and reaching agreement with the party who had possession of what you required, the ownership has now changed hands. In the business world it is necessary for those who run their business to account for their expenditure and their income to the government. Indeed, the people who are responsible for doing the books are even called accountants.

Accountability, however, relates not just to material, physical items but also to things that are unseen, such as emotions and energies. The law of karma is the accountant as it keeps tabs on all the positive and negative energies that are expended. The books are always perfectly balanced and there is no hiding from your debt. Every negative action must have a positive action in order for the books to be balanced to the accountant's satisfaction.

The Attic

Trapped
Like a bird in a cage
Caught up in something not totally understood
A bird has wings however
I have none
If a bar breaks the bird flies away
If a window breaks I must still stay
I can see a blue sky
And a pitched slate roof
I hear people's voices and the sound of traffic
But I am still here
In my solitary prison
People laugh
People shout with happiness
The joy of the company, the pleasure of the Sun on their faces
But I have no garden
No opportunity to walk on the streets
No one to walk with
I am alone
Trapped

Procrastination

Procrastination is the thief of time.

Edward Young

*H*ave you ever done this? Kept putting something off, over and over again even though you knew that it must be attended to? Made up the most outlandish excuses to yourself and to others just so that you could get out of what you had to do? I know I have. But where does it get you? Nowhere. It still has to be done and by the time you actually do it, the situation has become more difficult, people are angry and everything is just much harder to do. Add to that the fact that you have this continual heaviness inside you which doesn't go away, because you know that you have to do THIS THING, whatever it is.

At work it could be a job that is complicated and time-consuming, fraught with difficulties. You get to your workplace having told yourself that, today, you will deal with it. But then the phone rings. That's just an easy matter – "I can sort this out in a few minutes" – and so you do. Then someone unexpectedly calls in to see you. You see them. Then it's coffee time. Another few files land on your desk, but they're all simple matters. You tell yourself that it's far better to deal with these straight away and keep your desk nice and tidy. Then a colleague has a problem, so you help them with that. Then, guess what – it's lunchtime. While you're having your lunch there is this nagging in the back of your mind – you said you'd deal with that issue today and so far you haven't. "I promise I will," you tell yourself, "as soon as I get back to work."

When you get back there are some more phone calls for you to return and some more files on your desk. None of these is life-threatening or even important. In fact some of these are matters you could delegate, including the phone calls, but "no," you tell yourself – "it would be better if I attended to them." And then it's the end of the day. Another day when you have not dealt with this issue. Another day further down the line from when you should have delivered the goods. And how do you feel? Awful, guilty, pressurised and as if everyone who looks at you knows your terrible secret – you are a Procrastinator. "Never mind," you cheer yourself up – "I'll do it first thing tomorrow morning."

That night, you don't sleep so well. You have dreams whereby you are exposed. You are publicly humiliated. You are sacked. Life is no longer worth living. All because you failed to tackle something that you did not want to. You wake up feeling dreadful. You are tired. You have a headache. You feel slightly sick. Maybe I should have today off and then when I feel better tomorrow I can deal with this issue. If I try and do it today, I will make a mess of it. So you ring in and tell work you're sick. A little later your phone rings. It's a colleague asking where the file is, THE DREADED FILE, because, oh no, horror of horrors, the client has rung in and wants an update. "I've got the file here with me," you mumble. "Tell him I'll ring him tomorrow." The worst thing has happened. There is no escape.

You have to go to work, feigning some miraculous recovery, retrieve the file before anyone else can find it, lock yourself in your room with no phone calls allowed and a 'Do Not Disturb' sign on the door. You finally come to terms with tackling this difficult matter head on. Only now you have to be surreptitious about it. There is no way that you can openly seek other people's help and their opinions on it, because as far as everyone else is concerned, you have been working on it, you have everything under control.

Does some, or all, of this sound familiar to you? Why? Why do we do it to ourselves? Looking at the whole situation from a point of love, are we loving ourselves by allowing this to happen? Of course we're not. This is a case of feeling fear and deciding the best way to deal with it is to try to bury it, suppress it. But the only outcome of that is worry, anxiety, a continual gnawing inside us and ultimately illness. This is not the way we are meant to live our lives. This is definitely not loving ourselves.

So let's look at this scenario again. We are given something to deal with which causes us to feel uncomfortable. It causes us to doubt our abilities because we do not have as high an opinion of them as do the people with whom we work. We do not want to be seen to be a failure. Therefore we do our best to deny our discomfort and create all these excuses until, suddenly, time has run out for us. By loving ourselves we know that we must deal with this fear, this issue, straight away. We know it has to be addressed eventually and therefore it is so much better to deal with it immediately, when we have only just been given it, because at that stage, even though it is a challenge, it hasn't yet turned into the huge monster that it will become if not attended to.

Also, everyone will know that we have only been given the matter recently, so everyone's doors, including the clients' or customers', will be open for them to help us and contribute to the ultimate outcome. A phone call to the client/customer, speaking your truth and saying, "This is rather complicated so I have to investigate it – I can't therefore report back to you straight away," quietens his mind because he knows something is being done and it takes the pressure off you. You delegate all other matters as far as possible. You can receive all the help you need because you have given yourself the time and space to work in. You will find that from the wisdom you gain as you face this challenge, you will grow not only in knowledge but also in yourself as a person – all because of the way that you have dealt with this job. You will also become, or continue to be, a respected member of the team who can be handed challenging matters and who is not afraid to ask for help and to come up trumps.

It is our ego which prevents us from asking for help – in case we are considered to be ineffectual, it tells us. It doesn't, however, manage to give us any constructive advice to get us out of the mess we have got ourselves into. Simply because we are unable to come up with what was asked of us, we feel we have no other option but to tell lies.

If you really love yourself, why on Earth would you let yourself get into such a mess? You wouldn't, would you? So next time you are tempted to push something to the bottom of your pile of work, recognise it as a trigger and question yourself as to why you are doing it. And then follow it up with the question: "If I really loved myself I wouldn't want to give myself a hard time so what is the best thing for me to do for myself in this situation?" As you keep questioning your actions you will find that you are gradually changing without even realising it, and therefore there will be less and less need for you to question yourself about procrastination. You will experience the fear; recognise it as a challenge and learning opportunity, a means for personal growth, and deal with it straight away. After all, no one wants an ever-present monster hovering around them in their lives, always making them feel less capable than they should, discolouring their world and contaminating their opportunities for happiness.

We do exactly the same thing in our personal lives where relationships are concerned. We put off telling the other person the truth of what we are thinking and feeling. The excuses we use are "He/she might leave us and we don't want to be on our own." "He/she isn't perfect but it's better than being on my own." So we live a lie and become less than the person we really are. We don't grow; we shrivel away into our lies and our fears and become even less happy. What we have to realise is that, until we let go, nothing new can come into our lives. We hold on, thinking it can, but life will be tainted because we have not sorted out our baggage and, until we do, this will always have an adverse effect on any new relationship. The sayings "you can't make an omelette without cracking a few eggs" and "growth always follows the knife" are very true. So if we are holding on to something which is not right for us, we have to ask ourselves, again from a point of self love "Why are we allowing this to happen? Why are we letting ourselves live a substandard life instead of the life that we really want for ourselves?"

The reaction of your partner when you tell them the truth of who you really are, with gentleness and love, from one soul to another, may astound you. It will certainly trigger a response, which could either be an improvement in the relationship or could cause it to end. Either way it is going to be better for you than what you have now.

Very often we make the mistake of thinking that other people are mind readers. "They should have known," we say. "They should have guessed." Why? How? If we don't open our mouths and speak our truth, the people that we are in relationships with cannot know what we are thinking and feeling. Do you know what everyone you are having a relationship with thinks and feels? Of course you don't. It would be a miracle if you did. You need them to tell you so that if there are any misunderstandings they can be resolved. You need to know what they like so that you can plan special outings, meals, presents, that you know will please them and make them happy. So, speaking your truth is an essential part of your life and consequently of your relationships, whether professional or personal. Until the day my grandmother died she insisted on giving my dad sardines on toast. She was convinced as a small boy that he loved them and continued thinking that way even when he was an adult. She thought she was doing something special and loving for him. What she didn't know, because she was not a mind reader, was that he hated them, but didn't have the heart to tell her. It was a misconception, admittedly a harmless one, but, because my dad failed to tell her the truth, with the best motives in mind because he loved her and didn't want to hurt her, he had to find some way to dispose of the sardines on toast every time she gave them to him. I personally love sardines on toast!

I have a wonderful friend who is kind, loving and helpful to everyone. Her husband was a very controlling man with an addiction which caused great problems within their family life. Eventually she found the strength to make him leave the marital home. This was some years ago. Since then she has refused to let go of anything. She still wears her wedding ring, still lives in the same house and ultimately hoped that everything would resolve itself and the family would be reunited happily with no problems.

We can liken this situation to a guitar. When all the strings are at the right tension they resonate beautifully, creating a wonderful sound. But if only one of the strings is out of tune it causes a disharmony, and however precisely in tune all the other strings are the sound will always be jarring when the guitar is played with the string that is discordant. If the string is removed the guitar still won't play properly but it will have a more pleasing sound than before. And this is true of human relationships, especially in my friend's case. While her husband continued to be the discordant note, however much she wished it things could never be as they had once been. It could only happen if he addressed his issues and retuned himself.

Her husband now wants a divorce and even though she has gone as far as seeing a solicitor and commencing divorce proceedings, she is still dragging her feet. Life is trying to move forward for her, but because she is refusing to help it she is being pulled along slowly, full of negative emotions and not allowing any new doors to open for her. She has closed herself away securely behind her own walls, making herself a prisoner from all the pleasures that her life has to offer her. It's as if she is stuck in a bog and every time she lifts up a foot she allows it to be sucked back down into the same space. Close to where she is standing is a lovely dry solid earth bank and if she could just convince herself to walk out of the bog, she would find a whole new life waiting for her with many opportunities. But, because of her fear of what may be there she prefers to stick with what she knows, however bad it is, rather than move forward into the unknown. She acknowledges that she is procrastinating and also realises that at some stage she will have to climb out, but at the moment the bog is her security, however painful it may be to stay there. Following a recent conversation we had, she has now decided that to help her overcome her procrastination she is going to set herself time limits to deal with things – in other words, one step at a time. She has promised me that she will reach that bank!

Reactions to life's experiences are different for everyone. Some people move on quickly with their lives, others take longer. There is no right or wrong way. After all, it's your life and you are the one that has to live it. The only thing that I would say is that we never know, whatever age we are, how long we have on this Planet in our human form. It seems a shame, therefore, for us to take a long time to deal with major issues in our life by procrastinating. If we face our fears and deal with them they are never as bad as we think they will be. By dealing with them, we are liberating ourselves for the next phase and all the new things that the Universe can bring into our lives including peace, love and happiness. Procrastination prevents us from relinquishing that which we no longer need and so prevents us from moving forward.

Procrastination is indeed the thief of time. It deprives you of that which is rightfully yours. It holds you in a space where you do not wish to be and prevents you from moving into the space where you should be. You are kept in the dark by this negative energy instead of moving into the light, which is where your soul wishes you to be. By procrastinating, you are denying yourself the ability to truly be yourself. You are holding yourself back from becoming the truth of who you really are. You are allowing fear, a negative energy, to prevent you from stepping into that beautiful space which is yours and yours alone.

It is for you to recognise that the fear is there for a positive reason and therefore you must not react to it in a negative way but embrace it, welcome it and thank it for what it has come to teach you. By doing this, the experience will become a positive one, enabling you to blossom. Your growth will no longer be stunted. You will see the world, including yourself, through different eyes. Therefore, my child, do not procrastinate, do not delay, when your life could be so much better than it is. Recognise your ability to procrastinate and the limitations it will cause you. Deny it and move forward into the place where you are meant to be.

The Perpetrators

They came to us with their promises and their lies
They shared no respect for what was ours
They thought they could possess the land
They thought the yellow stuff belonged to them.

They took that which was not theirs
They raped the earth for the gold it bore
They killed our men so nothing would stand in their way
They took our freedom without a backward glance.

Who were they to think they were so much better than us?
What God-given right did they think that they had?
They lived with violence, fighting and death,
They had no concept of the Earth's peace and balance.

Instead of there being a sharing of knowledge
They assumed that they were right!
They caged us as they did the wild animals
Depriving us of our dignity and way of life.

Why did they possibly think they could own the Earth
And all the creatures above and below?
They have continued their legacy of destruction
Without understanding that they are destroying themselves.

They mocked the old ways
Thought of us as savages
But in the end we will see
Who lived in peace and harmony.

The land was our Mother, the sky our Father,
The rocks and trees our siblings.
We did not own anything, it was not our way,
We were blessed with their love and their bounty.

Freedom is living with love and understanding
Allowing others to be who they are
Knowing that everything we have is on loan to us
Ensuring the world's well-being for future generations.

But because of their greed and lack of understanding
Their arrogance and materialistic ways
Mother Earth is damaged, maybe beyond repair.
What now can their money buy?

Will it bring back the beauty of the land
Before it was raped and pillaged?
Will it bring back the birds and animals
Who have been brought to extinction?

All we can do is try to turn the time back
And live once again in harmony with Mother Earth
Appreciating and revering everything that lives
Inhabiting the land with the humans.

For we are all part of a delicate balance
And none is more important than another.
It is so necessary to learn to share for the good of all
Marvelling at the wonders of this mystical Planet.

Balance

As we look deeply within, we understand our perfect balance.
There is no fear of the cycle of birth, life and death.
For when you stand in the present moment, you are timeless.

Rodney Yee

*B*alance affects everything we do. We are awake and busy during the day and so need to rest and sleep at night to bring our energy back into balance. If there is playtime, there has to be quiet time. If there has been an excess of noise, your body clamours for peace. If you have been with a crowd, you desire some solitude.

We carry both male and female energies in us, the yin and the yang, and for us to be well-balanced human beings we need to carry equal amounts of energy – for the male energy is essential for us to be strong and courageous and the female energy is vital for creativity and compassion. If these energies are out of balance then this creates unbalanced situations, from which we need to learn so that our energies can be redressed.

Where a woman has too much feminine energy she places herself, due to her lack of self love, in a position where she is a martyr or can be abused, physically and mentally. This becomes such a habit that she starts to think that it is normal behaviour and it is only when she hears her inner self clamouring for attention that she finally does something about it. If she had loved herself in the first place this would not have happened, or if it had, she would have addressed it much more quickly.

One of my friends is definitely a martyr. She and her husband bought their home about 15 years ago. The kitchen was horrendous and as she is an excellent cook I looked forward to seeing how she would refurbish it. She had two small children, so first of all their needs had to be met, and then her husband's needs were met. Slowly they updated parts of the house, but each time her husband suggested doing the kitchen she said, "Oh no, I can manage. Let's do…" and would suggest something else that should be improved first. Then they ran out of money. So my dear friend is still cooking and spending a lot of time in a horrible, old-fashioned kitchen, when she could have had a brand new one, which would have been much easier to keep clean and would have been a pleasure for her to work in. She did not love herself. She put everyone else first.

I have also been a martyr to the cause in many things where my family are concerned, but the one that sticks in my mind was our ski holidays. My husband is an excellent skier and really loves his annual holiday in the mountains, so each year we and our two daughters would go skiing. They inherited their father's love of the sport and had ski lessons. This added to the cost of the holiday but I considered them to be an essential extra, from both a safety and a learning perspective. I was a mediocre skier who definitely needed more lessons but each year, because there wasn't enough money, I would agree to my husband having a few lessons and he would give me some coaching. He thought I didn't want any lessons. So everyone was learning to ski much better than I was, and this left me feeling resentful. I was quite happy about the girls having lessons but I couldn't see why my husband needed them when he was already such a good skier. This went on for years with them suggesting I should have lessons and with me refusing because I didn't think we could afford it, and being resentful. Then I started to love myself, and guess what, on the next ski holiday I had lessons. Well, I couldn't believe it. It was wonderful. I could ski so much better and my enjoyment of the sport and my holiday went up 100 per cent. To think I had put myself through so much grief by not loving myself, and it was no one's fault but my own. The knock-on effect is that my family are much happier, too, because they are enjoying me skiing with them, keeping up and really appreciating their sport. I can join in with what they're doing and see what they can show me. Best of all, there are no more temper tantrums on the slopes when my frustration at not being able to ski properly gets the better of me!

So why do we do this? Why do we condemn ourselves to live only a part of our lives, when we could be living the whole? The answer is so simple when you know. LOVE YOURSELF and by loving yourself you allow your energies to become balanced, embracing male as well as female.

Not only do we make ourselves victims by depriving ourselves of things which would make us much happier and more of a pleasure to be around, we also allow other people to make us their victims. A lady I met, who was well-educated, had reached the depths of despair because of her abusive husband. She had even gone so far as to contemplate suicide. When I spoke to her she did not know which way to turn, she had so many problems with every aspect of her life.

It has been scientifically proven that everything is made up of energy. We are energy that has been manifested and space is energy that has not yet manifested into any material object or life force. We are created by dense energy-forming matter that makes up what we are. When our human body dies, who we are, that is our energy, returns to the energy from whence we came. Energy never expands or decreases, it always remains the same.

When I channel through knowledge, advice and wisdom, I connect energetically with the energy around the person I am with. Some people describe it as my guides and angels speaking to the other person's guides and angels, and then giving me the information that needs to be shared with the other person to help them resolve their problems and move forward on their life's journey.

However, I always feel that my energy is connecting with a – or sometimes several – highly vibrating intelligent energetic beings, and this is where the loving guidance and knowledge comes from. I have never asked to be given a name, or names, for this intelligence as it would limit it to a level that our human minds can comprehend. In my opinion, this would be non-beneficial and be restrictive instead of opening up all the infinite possibilities that are out there that our minds haven't been able to grasp yet, but which our souls can comprehend.

The knowledge that I was able to channel through to her was loving and wise and it turned her life around. In short, she was told to concentrate on one problem only – whatever was most pressing. By doing this (and she was told how to deal with it) she was able to change those circumstances, and in changing them, every other situation changed in her life. She was then able to focus on the next pressing problem and deal with that in like manner. If you resolve issues one at a time you change who you are and, as a result of this, you look at the remaining matters through different eyes and see new ways to deal with them. Also, by sorting out just one thing at a time, you are relieved of the immense emotional pressure that you feel when you are trying to address everything at once. By taking her power back, she was no longer the victim, she was in control of her life and it made her feel so empowered.

Too much male energy is as destructive as too much feminine energy. When it is not balanced it can cause violence in a man and subservience in a woman, or the converse where a woman becomes bullying and domineering and a man becomes timid and afraid. For example, a man who has too much male energy feels that the only way he can control his relationships is by physical violence and mental cruelty. There are some women that do this too but it is generally men who resort to this treatment. They live in fear that their partner will leave them and so mete out punishment in case their fear materialises. In some cases they are caught in a spiral of depression and disgust at their own behaviour but their fear is all-consuming, which can result in the death of all parties concerned – the murder of those around him and the suicide of the murderer. His partner stays with him through fear and/or because she loves him and believes him every time he says he will change. Often she has nowhere else to go and thinks that, even if she did leave, he would find her and bring her back. Their relationship might then become more abusive and he could even harm the friends or family who had taken her in. She also stays because he has convinced her that no one else will want her. He destroys her self esteem. This element of control is one that the woman has been subjected to before, generally in this life as a child, although it could also be in a former life. This is why she has attracted this awful situation to her because she needs to clear it so that she can be free.

When we are subjected to a negative emotion we immediately go out of balance. We therefore need to look at this negative energy to see what positive action we can take to regain our equilibrium.

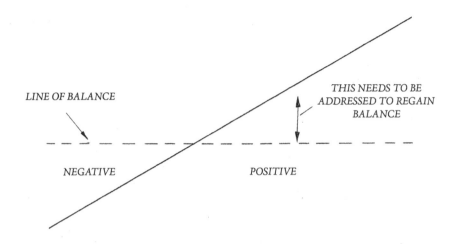

For instance, if we take the negative emotion of fear; some people live their lives full of fear, scared that they will lose everything they have. Unless they release this fear energy, they will indeed create both that which they are so scared of and in all likelihood also a physical illness. When we make decisions based on fear, the outcome is always negative and the wrong one for us, because we are not in the right space to make an enlightened choice.

The best way for us to respond to fear is to embrace it, because it is a prompt to show us what we need to learn. By dealing with it in a positive way we can bring ourselves back into balance. Treat it as your friend. I know this sounds strange but consider what fear actually means to us. The original reason for experiencing it was to trigger our fight or flight syndrome to facilitate our survival and the preservation of our lives and species. This fear was a short-term emotion, which then dissipated once the issue had been dealt with. Much of what we experience now, although still relating to our survival and preservation, is long-term worry. This is because we do not deal with our fears and instead try to suppress them. This is bad for our emotional well-being, the quality of our life and also our physical body, because the fear manifests itself as illness. However, if we address it as a lesson when we first experience it, we can resolve it and move forward. Our quality of life will improve and we will not make ourselves ill.

By failing to learn from your fear you just keep repeating the same circle, you complicate your life and do not allow yourself to live your dream. So greet your fear, welcome it and face it while it is still a molehill, before it grows into a mountain. It is the mind that feeds the fear, turning it into a veritable cyclone. The mind, in its misguided way, is attempting to protect you and tries to prevent you from hearing the truth that your heart is telling you with all its love, wisdom and compassion.

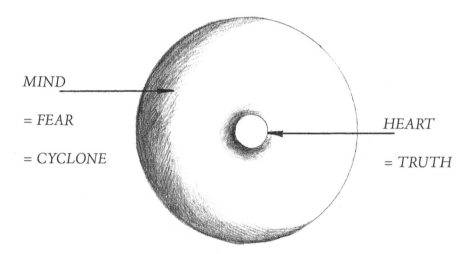

MIND

= FEAR

= CYCLONE

HEART

= TRUTH

Fear creates black spots in your life: depression, anger, bitterness, loneliness – all negative emotions. If you can sit and meditate, in other words go into your spiritual centre and not your mental one, and raise your vibrations, then you will receive guidance about what action to take. The answer may not be given to you immediately but it will come, so be on the look-out. It may come in the shape of some words being spoken, someone coming into your life who can help you, a situation arising which you react to, or in any number of forms. Challenge what you are given from a point of self love. If it survives your test then, armed with this knowledge, walk into your fear with complete trust and you will find it will crumble. When any worry is faced it is never as bad as the mind has led you to believe. You will find to your amazement that you have survived and that there is life on the other side. In fact, it becomes a good life because you have killed the monster and are now in a different space. If you had not opened yourself up to the glimmer of light that was being born from the darkness and bringing you the awareness you needed, you would still be stuck in the negative space of fear, sitting at the foot of the mountain, which just kept getting bigger all the time.

When everything is in alignment, there is no distortion, only balance.

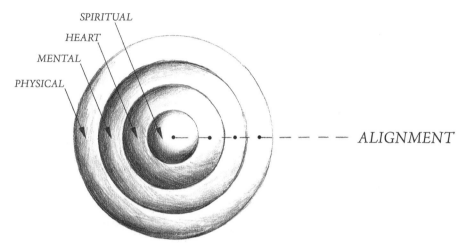

SPIRITUAL
HEART
MENTAL
PHYSICAL

ALIGNMENT

Remember, we all have good and bad in us, light and darkness, positive and negative. Out of the darkness, our negative emotions, comes our greatest growth. We need the dark to strengthen us and bring us into the light, into fruition. It is always our choice which pathway we take. There is no such thing as failure, only learning.

When we choose to be reborn, we bring back with us issues that happened in our former lives and have not yet been resolved. These are called 'karmic' issues and are negative matters that need to be dealt with in a positive way in this lifetime, so that balance can be regained. As you progress on your life's journey you will find that you have a number of karmic issues with the people in your life, as you will have been with them in several of your past lives. Each time a karmic issue is resolved, you are released from the detrimental energy that has prevented you from progressing. The beauty which you see around you is only a fraction of what is within you and of which you are a part. The more you free yourself from your past karmic issues and the negativity which tries to hold you back, the more beauty will come into your life to inspire and uplift you.

Karma is all about balancing the energy that has been created, whether in this life or past lives. If you hurt someone, physically or mentally, your action not only creates a negative energy towards the other person but also to yourself, because every action has a reaction.

Karma is about balance. It arises to bring the action that has taken place back into balance. If what has taken place is negative then a positive action is needed to rebalance it. This is of paramount importance for the whole concept of your life. Your edification as a human being is in bringing all aspects of yourself – personality, mind, heart, body and, as a result of this, your soul – into perfect balance, which ensures peace, love and harmony, this being the state that the soul wishes to be in permanently.

If you react violently to some person, injuring them either physically or mentally, then you will attract the same situation back to yourself, so that it can all be brought back into balance. The situation to you will not necessarily come from the person whom you have hurt; it may not even come in this lifetime, but it will happen, for the law of karma is perfect in this – everything has to be balanced energetically. This is why it is important that you are aware and take full responsibility for all your thoughts, words and actions. Every thought that you project will come back to you. Everything that you voice comes back to you. If you make a judgement of someone then someone else will be judgemental of you, and how can you judge someone else when you do not know what is going on in their life, mind, heart or soul, or why? You can of course comment on what they have done. For instance, if they have stolen then it is appropriate for you to say, "It is for the law to deal with this person," but it is not for you to say, "This is a bad person," for you are merely looking at it from the confines of your own humanity. You are not able to see the overall design. You may say, "But how do I know which way to go? How do I know what to do? I do not have any map or guidebook to explain these things to me." But you do. When you are born into this wonderful but challenging world, where each day is a lesson and each person you meet a test, you bring with you your soul, your consciousness, who you really are. Your memory is only with you for this life, as is this body, but your soul is with you for all time. It is part of the Universe and the Universe has full knowledge of all you need to do and know. It therefore brings everything into your life that is necessary, and when in doubt all you have to do is reconnect with who you really are and find out what your truth is – although I do acknowledge that this is not as simple as it sounds when you are in the middle of a challenge!

The victim and the bully are each victims in their own right, both lacking self love, because if either of them had self love they would immediately bring their role play to an end. Addicts are also people who are lacking in self love, apart from those who have tried alcohol or other drugs in a one-off experiment and their bodies have reacted strongly to them. Take the alcoholic for instance: his best day on booze is worse than his worst day when he was sober. All addicts suffer from their addiction, as do their families, because it is a family disease. To watch someone you love destroying themselves and not being able to do anything about it is heartbreaking. But the usual reason for their addiction is that there is something in their psyche that they do not wish to remember, and so they drink, take drugs, gamble, or do whatever it takes to kill or minimise the pain. Initially it works, but then they need more and more to satisfy the cravings of their body. Ultimately, unless they decide they need help or they are prepared to accept help when it is given to them, they commit a slow and debilitating suicide. The help that is available would show them how to face their pain and move on from the cause of their addiction. It would allow them to look at themselves in a different way, and in some cases to love themselves and so bring about a balance. However, as with everything else in life, it is their choice.

Often, when we think we have learnt our lesson, it crops up again just to make sure we really have. It is interesting at that stage to see how we react. We will either recognise the situation and move away from it, knowing it for what it is and being adamant that we do not want to go through that learning curve again, or we may not hear the alarm bells ringing until we have started to repeat our old pattern. The reassuring thing, though, is that if we have learnt our lesson, we will quickly hear the sirens and realise that we have to get out of the situation we have got ourselves into or deal with it in a completely different way. It is always great when you recognise the lesson and resolve the issue differently from before.

In April 1999 I was inspired to write the following, which I feel is right to share with you here. It was following a meditation in which I was shown an egg in two halves:

"Half (of the egg) symbolises learning spiritually and (the other) half symbolises learning in a worldly sense. This makes a balanced whole. Too much of one and not enough of the other, whichever way, leads to a damaged soul. You are made up of both worldly and spiritual parts and it is as important that you develop both these sides equally and in harmony.

"Except in special instances, it is important that you do not withdraw from the world and its people, and use its worldly experiences to enhance your spiritual side and vice versa. It does not do the soul any good if it has too much spirituality or too much worldliness. There are an enlightened few who choose to live away from the world but for them this is the right choice, because their knowledge is such that the world has nothing to teach them. There are others, however, who choose to ignore the world and only pursue a spiritual path. They become ill as they have not yet progressed far enough and need the balance of both, to learn and be well.

"If your life becomes unbalanced then this manifests itself in both physical and mental illnesses. This is disabling both for the person concerned and for those around them.

They are no longer in a position to be able to move forward and develop, or help to teach those around them. It is therefore essential that they look at their life and see where the imbalance is and then correct it.

"It is right, therefore, for you to live your worldly life, having experiences and enjoying it, while you are also living your spiritual life. Indeed, at the stage you are at, you cannot develop properly without both, as your worldly experiences open you up to your spiritual life and your spiritual life helps you to deal with situations which arise in your worldly life.

"So you see, my child, it is important that neither side is neglected and both sides must bring you enjoyment and learning. You are meant to be in perfect balance and harmony with all of nature and everything around you, which includes the spiritual, and it is when this is not the case that your energies are low and life appears to be a constant battle. When this happens, go and sit quietly, ask for guidance and look at the balance of these two things – your worldly side and your spiritual side. You can see all this just looking at the people you know – you can see who are balanced and who are not."

Balance is all. It is the rising of the Sun and the setting of the Sun in all its splendour. It is the cold in one part of your Planet and the heat in another part. It is life and death. It is sickness and health. It is male and female. It is positive and negative. When things are in balance they just are. People in balance go with the flow and embrace all that comes to them. But when one is out of balance, then there are difficulties. That is when the mirror that reflected such a beautiful image is cracked and now reflects distortion. Balance is the way in which to live your life, and the pathway you walk creates these challenges, which are all about bringing your soul into harmony, into the perfect balance, into the world of being where all aspects of your personality, heart and soul are in complete and total balance.

A Perfect Love — My Wish

My love for you fills my heart and soul
And causes me to vibrate at a level
Higher than I would have believed possible.
I know by your smile, touch, caress,
That you feel the same resonance.

Individually we are nothing,
Just two incomplete halves, or even less,
But together we are complete, total.
We encompass the universe in our embrace,
Our love enables us to blend, become one.

We share one heart, one soul,
The same total depth of feeling and emotion.
We resonate on a higher frequency
Radiating our light and love
Like some miraculous ever-burning circle.

Together we can climb mountains,
Build bridges, walk through fire,
Feel completely secure knowing we have found where we belong,
A place where we are never condemned, only welcomed,
Never belittled, only supported.

As we walk our pathway, we touch ourselves and others
With our wonderful love and inner peace.

Happiness

If there were in the world today any large number of people who desired their own happiness more than they desired the unhappiness of others, we could have paradise in a few years.

Bertrand Russell

*L*oving yourself happens on two different levels. The first level is your human self – that is, your body and your personality. Instead of dwelling on what you don't like about yourself, look at what you have got to be happy about. Instead of constantly running yourself down, love your good points and then start looking at what you consider to be your bad points with love and sympathy and see if there is anything you can do about them. If there is and it will make you feel better, then do it; if not, try to accept them. However, it could be that only you consider them bad points. Others may not have even noticed them or may like them because it is what attracts them to you. It could be what makes you unique. What you really need to do is look at the real reason you consider them to be bad points. Do you think that if you change your appearance you will immediately become popular and have the perfect life? I'm sorry, but that's not the case. If you were to ask the person who you thought had everything that you wanted whether they considered their life to be perfect, the answer would be "no." The reason for this is that you are only looking at things from an outsider's point of view. You know about all the turmoil and churning that is going on inside you with your life's problems but what you fail to realise is that the same emotions are going on inside everyone else. Money cannot buy happiness; beautiful looks cannot create happiness. Happiness is something that is worked at and achieved.

There is a difference between fairy-tale happiness and real happiness. Fairy-tale happiness can be taken away because there is no real depth to it – it is a façade but one that is being lived as though it were true. When any problems arise to confront this dream they will be suppressed, because the person living this life will be frightened in case the challenge is strong enough to break the vision, like a breeze blowing over a house made from a pack of cards. But it is doomed anyway, because once the element of fear has been introduced, however much it is ignored, it won't go away and, like a cancer, it will keep eating away at the dream until the fear is faced or the fantasy is destroyed. The fear has to be faced at some stage, whether before or after the destruction of the dream, and either way, the person will have to start looking at the situation realistically. In doing this they will grow personally and end up with a genuine set of circumstances. Real happiness is created by accepting yourself for who you truly are, not criticising but loving and giving yourself support. Others may criticise you so you don't need to knock yourself down as well, and let's face it, when you criticise yourself you can do it every minute of the day!

When situations arise, stop and look at them. Think about what you can learn. Think what you have done to create this state of affairs. Acknowledge the fear that you are feeling. Then think about how you can resolve this in the most loving and harmonious way possible for yourself. If you have difficulty doing this, imagine it is your best friend who is asking you for advice. You would only ever give them a loving solution, so give it to yourself. If you do this, if you walk your pathway of truth and self love, you will learn the lessons which are being given to you and, each time, your feelings of happiness and security will grow. This will not only be good for you: it will be good for those around you because you will be coming from a different space and that will help them too. Not only are people in our life for us to learn lessons from them – we are in their lives for the same reason.

The second level is your soul – who you really are. The soul continues forever but your body will die and your personality with it. Your immortal soul decides what it needs to heal and thereby creates the appropriate body and personality for its experiences, with the heart being the instrument of the soul. By restricting ourselves to only existing as human beings with personalities and minds we are limiting our amazing abilities and the purpose of our lives. We are so much more than we appear to be on a visual level. We are life; we are energy and as such can connect with other sources of energy. Consider all the life forces on this Planet including Mother Earth herself. We are all one and interconnected. If we hurt anything or anyone we are also damaging ourselves. We need never feel alone or insecure because we are unique and we are meant to be here. We are as important a part of the chain of life as anyone or anything else.

Everything and everyone has their own beauty – not an external, artificial beauty but the internal beauty of the soul. This beauty can sometimes be very well hidden due to the learning that particular being is going through, but they are the ones who need us to send them light and love more than the ones whose beauty we can see, because they are the ones who have got lost along the way. They are the ones who have no self love. They are the ones whose hearts have been completely taken over by negative emotions. But remember, out of the dark comes light. It has always been the case. There is a spark of light, hidden deep within which is the soul, and with correct nurturing it can show itself. Light was created from the darkness of the Universe; new life comes from the darkness of the ground, womb, shell, into the light. Stories told by people who died and then came back to life tell how they went through a dark tunnel and there was a brilliant light at the end. And then there is the saying "the darkest hour is just before dawn." How many of us have experienced that? The whole world is closing in on us and just as we are about to go under, something happens, a glimmer of light, which gives us hope, gives us something to work towards.

The cicada is, in my opinion, an unattractive bug, but it sings all through summer and its sound is synonymous with good weather, blue skies, sun, holidays; in other words, the feel good factor. Every living thing has its own vibration: for instance, mountains vibrate very slowly and cicadas vibrate much faster than us human beings. I went to a talk given by Barry Brailsford in Auckland a few years ago and he told us how he had recorded the song of the cicadas. He then slowed their vibration down until it was the same vibration at which we resonate and played their song to us. It was one of the most beautiful sounds

I have ever heard. These ugly bugs sounded like a choir of angels, singing their songs in perfect harmony. It had a real ethereal quality to it and it was difficult to believe that an insect was capable of choreographing such music. Indeed, on one of the walks which I take, I pass through a tunnel of trees and the cacophony of the cicadas is deafening. But because I know what they really sound like on my vibrational level, I feel very privileged to hear their music and it makes me feel as though I am in a special spiritual place where the angels sing. What this means is that nothing is as it seems. And it is for us to look deeply to observe what we are meant to see and then enjoy the beauty that is revealed. It is not for us to limit ourselves and our lives to the outer experience. It is for us to blend and be at one with all things, knowing that in their own way nothing is inferior or superior to us and we must treat everything and everybody with reverence, especially our own self.

Already we know what complex beings we are, and that our body functions on its own without any help from us provided we feed, water and exercise it appropriately – just as we would our car! I remember when I was pregnant I could not get over the fact that my body, without any help from me as a person, was creating a baby, a little human being, that was going to be born with its own looks, personality, thoughts and brain. It was mind-blowing! It was a good job my body knew how to do it, because I wouldn't have had a clue. Life is so precious, it is such a gift, and therefore it is in our best interests to use our time wisely, in as loving and positive a way as possible, so that we can learn as much as we can and ultimately live a life of peace, happiness, contentment and love.

Happiness is the chuckle of a baby, the laughter of a child, the response of an animal to an act of kindness. Happiness is seeing all the wonderful colours of a rainbow after the dark clouds have taken away the light and you have been drenched in the rain, when this beauty suddenly and without warning appears in the skies. Happiness is the joy when the newly born are seen for the first time – whether it be the human child, the bird breaking its shell, the lamb emerging into the day, the foal struggling to stand, the small seedling thrusting itself through the soil, the snowdrops heralding that the winter is about to end and the spring start. It is their sheer innocence which touches your inner core and brings about those feelings of happiness, and all these are natural occurrences. None of them is from the lower levels of materialism but all are from the higher energies of creation. Happiness is when joy builds inside you and it grows and becomes fluid, until you can no longer hold it within and it flows from you, touching all who are in its path. Happiness is a gift of the Universe. When you are lucky enough to have received it, look after it and make constant use of it. It is indeed a blessing from the heavens and those that carry it attract others who are anxious to receive the same.

Truth and Distortion –
The Debate

At one end is truth
At the other end distortion
And I am the pendulum which swings between the two.

I started with truth
But as I embraced the ways of the world
I distorted myself to impress others.

The more distorted I became
The more my truth cried out.
My choice was to ignore it and live in the world.

The distortion I saw as myself
Instantly attracted others who, too, were distorted,
And we played into each other's projected roles and images.

One day I realised the grief I was causing
Not only to myself but others;
For in not walking my own truth
I was confusing those around me,
I was teaching them by example not to walk in their truth.

So looking and admiring the truth of youth
I slowly started honouring myself
And began the ascent back to who I truly am.

The pain that I have felt between my breasts
For more years than I care to remember
Is slowly receding as my body reacts to the truth.

How could I have treated myself so badly?
– Because I wanted to fit in.
All this need created, however, was someone that I was not.

It has taken so long to recognise this lesson,
So much difficulty and misery in between,
But at last with much help I am learning.

It is slow to begin after many years in denial,
However, with each truth my heart leaps with joy
And I feel so much stronger.

I feel courageous as my truth is accepted,
I start to remember who I truly am,
And in doing this I clarify the confusion that I had created around me.

So my dear brothers and sisters,
Do not listen to your mind, only your heart.
Be not afraid to be the truth of who you really are,
For that person is infinitely more beautiful and at peace
Than any distortion that you think you should be.

Truth

Men occasionally stumble over the truth, but most of them pick themselves up and hurry off as if nothing ever happened.

Sir Winston Churchill

*M*any business people have problems in their personal relationships. To be successful they have used their minds, which they feel comfortable doing, and their power in negotiating deals. Because they are using their intellect, they say whatever needs to be said to get the best deal for themselves, their clients or their customers. This gives them a sense of excitement and an addictive buzz when they achieve the outcome they want. However, it does not involve their hearts. The heart, as well as being the organ that pumps the blood around our body keeping us alive, is the emotional core of our being and is at one with our soul. It needs nourishment so that it does not shrivel up and become diseased; it needs truth and love, from others and, especially, from ourselves.

Imagine your heart as a tiny bud. Every time you speak your truth it starts opening up, ultimately destined to be a beautiful flower, but when you lie it closes up again and becomes damaged. People who are used to getting what they want in the business world bring their mind, with its knowledge, into their personal life and as a result continually say what they think other people want to hear, or what they think gives them the best result, rather than speaking their truth. As like attracts like, they attract others who are also telling lies. Therefore the lesson in all of this is to speak your truth from the heart with love, wisdom and compassion.

To put this diagrammatically: imagine you are a straight line in your most beautiful and truthful state, the state in which you should try to be in all the time (Line A). Line B occurs when you have told a lie and, as you continue along that pathway, you tell another lie (Line C). The same scenario happens again, which brings us to Line D and so on. Look at the distance you have moved away from your true self. Therefore, you will attract a person who has also moved away from the truth of who they really are, so that you can learn this lesson (see diagram on opposite page).

We create what we need in our own lives by attracting the people to us who can give us the lessons we need to learn. I call this the Mirror Image Syndrome (see diagram on page 108).

When something in our partner, parents, children, friends or even a stranger really annoys us, we have to look at ourselves to find out what it is in us that is causing us to react in this way. Instead of being angry with them we can be grateful to them for 'pushing our buttons.' We can then work on the issue that has been brought to our attention, and we will know that we have dealt with it successfully when the same situation arises and we do not react to it. This is our learning path.

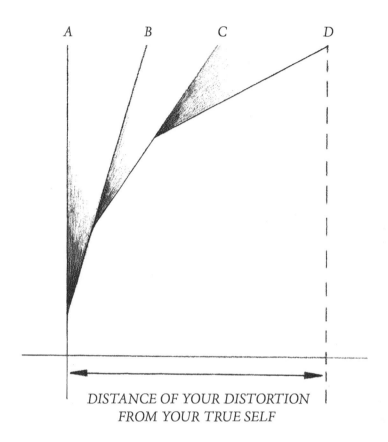

DISTANCE OF YOUR DISTORTION
FROM YOUR TRUE SELF

We are fearful of telling the truth because when we were children we would get into trouble for doing so, classics being, "Mummy, why is that lady so fat?" or "Mummy, look at that ugly man." The keywords here for telling our truth are love, wisdom and compassion. Most of us want to be liked and we would wish to have as simple a life as possible with few arguments and few hardships. Because of our fear we react in various ways. We either succumb to what another person wants, suppressing who we truly are deeper and deeper; we become confrontational and argumentative which, depending on the strength of the person we are having our dispute with, will result in us either winning or losing; or we may take on a bullying mentality and ensure we win whatever it takes, such as getting groups of people to support us by ganging up on the other person, telling lies about them, or even physically assaulting them.

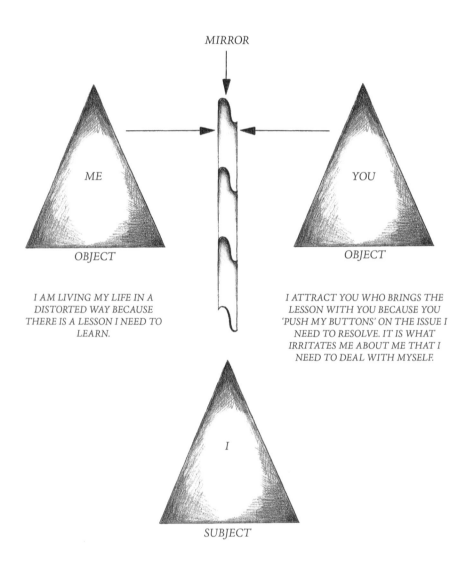

MIRROR

ME

YOU

OBJECT

OBJECT

I AM LIVING MY LIFE IN A DISTORTED WAY BECAUSE THERE IS A LESSON I NEED TO LEARN.

I ATTRACT YOU WHO BRINGS THE LESSON WITH YOU BECAUSE YOU 'PUSH MY BUTTONS' ON THE ISSUE I NEED TO RESOLVE. IT IS WHAT IRRITATES ME ABOUT ME THAT I NEED TO DEAL WITH MYSELF.

I

SUBJECT

THE RESULT OF THE LEARNING IS THAT A LAYER OF MY DISTORTION HAS BEEN REMOVED ENABLING ME TO BE TRUER TO MYSELF THAN BEFORE.

All these are negative scenarios and are based on the regime of personal power. The strong will lead and the weak are suppressed and their opinions are not worth listening to. This is not the right way forward in a relationship and certainly brings no peace of mind for the parties concerned, either short or long term, because no one is speaking and consequently living their truth. So what is it that drives us to behave like this? It's our old friend fear again. The bully boy is relieved he's won: he cannot bear to think what would happen to his street credibility and subsequently himself if he lost. The suppressed party becomes more of a victim and increasingly fearful of anyone who might try to impose their will on them. After all, "It's a jungle out there"; "Everyone for themselves"; "Dog eat dog." WRONG. This is not the way to live our lives the way we truly want to live them. Sit down quietly somewhere and write a list of all the things you want for you in your life that will make you happy and will give you the life that you would choose for yourself. Then look at it and see if you can understand why you haven't got them. How many times have you ended up with something that you didn't really want because you didn't want to hurt someone's feelings or because you allowed them to overrule what you really wanted? Maybe you lie because it's just easier than telling the truth – anything for a quiet life! Maybe you are deluding yourself and have suppressed the fact, successfully, that you are not telling the truth?

What you have to remember is that every time you tell a lie, you are not only failing to love yourself but you are also causing damage to yourself both mentally and, over a long time, physically as well. The mind is very smart – it will give you all types of reasoned arguments why you should say and do certain things, but the danger is that if it is in conflict with your heart and your soul, in other words your truth, then a battle starts being waged inside you, ultimately resulting in illness if nothing changes.

When you have lied for a long time it becomes a habit and the concept of telling the truth seems very difficult. Indeed, some people have lied so much that they have convinced themselves that they are telling the truth and that it is everyone else who is telling lies. Start in small ways. Practise telling the truth, but always lovingly, and see what happens. You see, in lying to yourself and to others you are portraying a false image of who you really are and you are attracting people who are also portraying a false image of themselves. What are you frightened of? That your whole world will come tumbling down? Surely it is far better to live an honest, truthful life based on self love with others who do the same. It creates much deeper, worthwhile, loving relationships with people who say exactly what they mean and how they feel. By speaking your truth there will be at least one person you know that this will help. You may ask me how? By always lying to them you have condoned them lying to you and to themselves. Therefore, your relationship (and when I use this word I mean your relationship with anyone you know, be it parent, sibling, child, friend, colleague or acquaintance) is built on falsehoods. By speaking your truth to them you will start pushing their buttons, which will help them to begin clearing the cloud of negativity they carry around with them and walking their pathway of truth.

Many relationships between people, especially couples, carry on with each of them lying to the other, in fear – there's that word again! – that if they actually told the truth, the relationship would end, that the other person would recoil in horror. Very often what happens is that if one of them starts telling the truth in an honest and loving way and not in order to score points or retaliate, it opens the door for the other to also start telling the truth, and gradually all the lies can be cleared away. A deeper and more meaningful relationship can be the result, not only with each other but also with themselves. The biggest fear of telling the truth is the fear of rejection by the other person. Also, there is the knowledge that actually speaking words of truth will be very difficult and painful, especially if you have been lying for a long time.

I had a strange experience in a situation where I had been lying to my husband for some time. It was a pretty big lie. I'd been having an affair with a married man. I hated the mess I'd managed to get myself into, the lies, the cheating, the emotional state I was in, the continual seesaw of emotions and, worst of all, the effect that it would have on my husband and daughters and our relationships if and when it came out. My husband and I had gone out for a drink one evening and were sitting in a bar when I suddenly heard the words inside my head that I had to say to him. I tried to ignore what was being said to me but they just became more insistent. Then it was as though the whole world stopped and everything was holding its breath. I could no longer hear the music or people talking, even though the bar was crowded and the music was playing quite loud. I just knew that nothing would move again until I spoke these words. It felt so weird, as though time had stopped. So in the end I did the only thing I could do: I told the truth, and the world started again. It was the beginning of my journey back onto the pathway that I should have been walking. Obviously I had to deal with the consequences of the words I had spoken, but it was such a relief to no longer be lying that I was able to cope with the way that my husband reacted and the questions he asked. Whatever the outcome when you speak your truth, and even though at the time it may not feel like it, it will always be the one that is right for you. It will always be the one with your highest and best interest at heart.

Take the scenario of the successful businessman who is having an ongoing affair – and as you know, my insight comes from personal knowledge. He is lying to his wife but there are obviously problems within the marriage, because otherwise he would not be able to find the energy or time to sustain this other relationship. His wife is lying to herself that everything in their marriage is fine, while deep down she knows that it is not because he will have disclosed it in many little signs. However, she has chosen either not to see these signposts, or to ignore them. The mistress is also lying to herself about the relationship, by thinking that all the sneaking around and snatched meetings are worth it just to be able to spend some time with him. She knows that when it comes to Christmas, family holidays, birthdays, etc, she will always come second. If she is married, then she is also lying to her husband, however justified she might feel in having the affair, and her husband is lying to himself by putting his head in the sand or by choosing, subconsciously or consciously, not to see the signs. Therefore these four people, by their chosen lies, can keep this relationship going indefinitely until something happens to upset the balance, such as the couple having the affair getting bored with each other, one or both of them deciding they want to make it a full-time relationship, or one of the spouses deciding they want to challenge the situation.

The other people to take into consideration are the children of the respective couples. Children, like animals, are very aware of changes in atmosphere, voice tones and energy vibrations. They can detect when adults are lying and it confuses them, because they have always been told to tell the truth. They are already confused about the truth issue, as I mentioned earlier, because they are no longer too sure when it should be spoken and when it shouldn't. Therefore, this situation adds to their confusion. It also shows them that it is acceptable to lie and cheat, not just generally but to the person that is supposed to be the closest to you, the person who is your spouse or partner.

So just stop and think this scenario through from everyone's point of view. The couple having the affair, instead of talking through the shortcomings of their respective marriages with their spouses and facing the fear that it could mean the end of their relationship, and instead of looking at positive means of addressing their problems and improving their marriages, they find it easier to seek the heady excitement of a relationship with someone else. For her it is probably because she feels unloved and unappreciated at home and for him it could be the same, although in some instances it could be because he feels that he's got the business, the house, the wife, the car, and the next thing on his list is the mistress. I hasten to add that this could also be true of a successful businesswoman, not just a businessman. The spouses who are being cheated on fear that if they confront their partners it will bring their marriages to an end, although if a time for confrontation arises it usually becomes a power struggle, which embraces all types of negative qualities. For the children, there is the fear that their mum and dad will split up if they say anything, and there is also the mistaken lesson that it is acceptable to lie. So these are the negative, fear-based outcomes.

If, however, we look at a truth-based scenario, where truth is told with love and compassion, it results in a much more positive outcome, embracing honesty and the chance for a better and happier life. Firstly, the mistress needs to look at herself with self love and ask whether she deserves better than what she is getting out of her affair. The answer has to be "yes." We all deserve to have a loving, honest and open relationship. Then, whatever she decides, whether it's to leave her husband and be with her lover, end her affair to be with her husband (if she has one), end the affair, or leave both of them to live on her own, she must tell the truth with compassion, knowing that that is what's right for her. In telling her truth, not only does she free herself but she frees all the others in the situation to confront their own issues and truths, and either deal with the problems honestly or fall back into a relationship based on lies that is never going to be successful or happy. It is up to each individual to be responsible for their own choice.

I'm just so grateful that the Universe pushed me into a situation where I had to tell the truth. There was a lot of sorting out, much heart-searching on everyone's side, and many painful emotions of anger, hurt and rejection to deal with, but eventually I and my family managed to work everything through and move on together, each one of us learning valuable lessons, especially about the importance of telling the truth.

It is during the times of challenge in our lives when we grow as an individual; it is never when all is calm and going well. If a relationship is worth having, then it's worth working at it and facing the fear that telling your truth will change things. It can only change things for the better. If the marriage is worth saving it can be worked on and will be better and exist on a deeper level as a result of its challenge. If it ends, then you are liberated to walk your pathway of truth and attract someone who is also walking the same pathway. The children are not to be ignored either in these situations. They also fear the unknown and need to be told the truth and reassured. They need to know that adults can make mistakes and that telling lies is not right because of the damage it does, not only to others but also to the ones who are lying. They need to be told to always speak their truth with love, compassion and wisdom.

Everything happens for a reason and the reason is us. We attract what we put out so if we only put out positive thoughts, love ourselves and speak our truth gently but with love, then this is what we will attract. Our minds have ruled us for too long. Now is the time for us to walk in trust, knowing that everything that comes to us is what we need for our own learning. Let us trust in the loving, compassionate influence that some call God, Allah, Jehovah, Elohim etc but which I prefer to refer to, all-embracing, as the Universe.

The more often you tell your truth, starting with small truths, the more you will realise that that is the only way to live and the easier it will become for you. Indeed, if you then begin to tell a lie, your body will physically react and you will feel a churning in your stomach. You will also notice a difference in the quality of your life. But remember, "you can't make an omelette without breaking a few eggs."

It is important to be as childlike, not childish, as you can. Children look at things with wonder and explore without fear. They have not yet had their minds tarnished with negativity. If we can copy what they are and we once were, we will find living so much easier. We know we will only attract what we need and that we are to look at things as an exciting adventure, knowing that there is no such thing as failure, only learning and growing. In that way fear has no hold over us, whatever our mind tries to tell us, and we free ourselves to walk our pathway in our own truth, which we share with others with love, compassion and wisdom. Loving ourselves frees us to do this and to live a better life. Before we ever make a decision about anything in life, we have to ask ourselves, "Because I truly love myself, which choice has the highest and best outcome for me?" This way you will never make the choice which will only give you second best. This way you will not have regrets.

When you speak your truth it has an undeniable ring to it, and others are silent for a few moments before speaking because they are aware of the irrefutability, to you, of what has just been said and it connects with something deep down inside them – their truth.

When words of truth are spoken from one to another they have a special vibration, a resonance that connects the core of the one being with the core of the other by means of a golden thread of light. The soul that is speaking knows that it is speaking its truth, for in doing so it feels balanced and knows that the right outcome will prevail because of these words that are being spoken. The receiver of the words feels their effect resonating within his core and affecting him energetically. His truth recognises and greets the truth from the other soul. Because of this recognition the response will ultimately only come from the source, for the Universe is all that is truth, love and beauty, and, indeed, only vibrates on the higher levels. It vibrates with such intensity that you in the human form can have no concept of what it is able to achieve. But when truth is spoken between two souls, this is the closest awareness that you can experience while in human form.

Therefore, in order to be connected as much as possible to the wonderful energies of the heavens, ensure that at all times you speak your truth and in so doing you will attract others to you who do the same.

An Affair – The Aftermath

I despise you
But not as much as I despise myself
I said no in the beginning
Because we were both married
But you wore down my resistance
No – correction
I allowed you to wear down my resistance
I have to accept the joint responsibility.

We called it love
What a fine love
One that cheats, that lies
We excused ourselves because we were in love
LOVE
How can that word be used when it destroys
Our husband, wife and children
They trusted us
They believed us
And we let them down in the name of love.

We ignored their love
Their selflessness, their trying to keep their marriages on track
Plodding on regardless
Knowing they were doing it on their own
Now, however, I see things with clarity
I see you for what you really are
And I see who I truly am
The fantasy dream has disappeared
I see the reality.

I see the love of my husband and children
Despite everything I have done
Why did I not see this before?
Why did I not treasure and value their love as I should?
LOVE
Now I see the true meaning of the word
Its beauty, truth and depth
Not the cheapening secret lying world
Where we used this word as our excuse.

So before you snatch stolen moments
Before you have your secret kisses
Before your smouldering passion makes you take leave of your senses
Engage your true heart and see if your actions are good enough for you
And good enough for those who truly love you
Remember it could just be a fantasy
With far-reaching destructive effects on innocents.

Desire

I count him braver who overcomes his desires than him
who overcomes his enemies.

Aristotle (384 BC–322 BC)

"I want" is desire, whereas "I need" is necessity. You may want that dress but what does that tell you about your needs? Do you want the dress because you think it will make you look good? Yes, but for how long will it make you feel that way? Is it a quick fix of happiness or something additional to the happiness you already feel? If it is the latter then there is no problem with you succumbing to your desire, provided of course you can afford it. However, if it only provides you with a quick fix you need to look deeper into yourself and find out where your real happiness lies. Maybe you feel that in buying that dress you will feel attractive and your partner will be loving to you again, or if you are alone maybe you think the dress will attract someone to you. When the dress does not have the desired affect then you may feel depressed again. Remember, you attract back what you put out.

Desire is our temptation, our challenge. Many wrong-doings are carried out in the name of desire. Women desirous of successful and wealthy men as partners marry them with no love, or have affairs with them because of the material items that they can get. Men desirous of feeling good about themselves like to be seen with an attractive, well-dressed lady because they feel that reflects well on them and their status in life, especially when they are getting older and their companion is young. When their wives no longer treat them as though they are special they have affairs with women who make them feel great about themselves. We all desire the passionate love that we read about and when our own relationships fall short we look to find it with someone else.

Burglaries are committed by thieves who are desirous of another's belongings, either because they covet them for themselves, or because they can sell them and make money without having to work. Desire can cause one person to murder another in the mistaken belief that they will escape justice and achieve what they want. If you look at the animal kingdom, you will see that by and large it functions on a need basis – the need for food, shelter and warmth. Animals live in harmony and balance unlike man who has upset his. But we are here to learn and this is part of our learning process. The truth is simple but very often we have complicated it, because we feel there have to be explanations involved or we feel we cannot speak our truth because of the effect it will have on others. In order to love ourselves truly, the only way that we can live is to speak our truth lovingly to others and to ourselves. Next time we decide we want something we have to decide whether it is a desire or a need, or a desire covering up a need.

Desires are usually the exact opposite of what we need. Desire is the inner naughty child enticing us away from what we know we should be doing. It only ever gives us short-term satisfaction because it is not fulfilling our need, and very often our action in satisfying our desires hurts others, makes us culpable and creates karma for us. However, we can learn much from following the pathway of desire if we subsequently reflect on what we did and what caused the desire in the first place. But, as always, when we pursue our self examination we must do it from the perspective of self love, knowing that it is not for us to criticise ourselves: it is for us to learn.

A friend of mine, who had an affair, realised that she had been following a pathway of desire – she was attracted to his success and his wealth, which meant that he could take her to wonderful places and buy her beautiful things. However, he could not satisfy her need for his company when she wanted it, not just when he was available. Her heart needed a relationship with a partner who was reliable, supportive, available, loving and able to commit himself to her 100 per cent. By examining the relationship from a point of self love she realised he was merely a 'want', a 'desire', he was not a 'need', a 'necessity'. She realised, coming from self love, that she deserved better; she deserved what she needed, which was infinitely more satisfying for her than what she wanted.

Desire has a very strong pulling power; it makes itself so attractive to you. It dresses up in such a way that you think you will die if you don't have it and, if you are unable to satisfy it, you can become obsessive about your wish to fulfil The Desire. It is so easy to mistake desire with need because such strong emotions are involved, usually heady, excitable emotions, and they override anything that anyone says to you, whether they are well-meaning friends, partners, parents or children. Desire does not bring completeness, fulfilment, peace, happiness or joy – all long-term positive emotions. Desire has to be continually satiated, appeased, dealt with – otherwise there are periods of emptiness, loneliness, grief and sadness, not to mention the time spent and energy wasted planning how you are next going to satisfy its demands. It is a negative draining emotion and energy, and takes over your life, making you dissatisfied with what you do have.

Need complements what you already have and indeed allows you to go deeper into the rich tapestry of your life and your emotions. Sometimes, when a desire is looked at in detail, it can be recognised as a need. For instance, wanting the new dress is actually a need to be loved. Wanting to go to America for 12 months could be an inner need, because we know that this is the right pathway for us as it will take us out of our comfort zone and allow us to grow. It will also enable us to meet new people, and have experiences which could change the direction of our life.

By expressing a need from the heart you are speaking your truth. As a result, even though it may be difficult to say and painful for others to hear, because of the energies that are used the dynamics will change between speaker and listener as a result of the vibrations of the words that are spoken. It may not happen immediately, as both of you will need time to absorb what has been said and to address your emotions but it will definitely bring about a transformation between you. The truth is the most powerful thing that can be spoken, because it comes from your love centre. It is you looking after and loving yourself enough to be able to be able to say what has to be said. It also makes it easier for you to deal with the situation if you remember you have created it and there is a learning experience in it for you. It may even be the resolving of a karmic issue. So, by speaking your truth, you address what is happening to you, which in turn affects other people's behaviour as they recognise at a deeper level the meaning of your truth and respond from that space. If you fail to speak your truth, whether you say nothing or deviate from the truth, the energy that is being created between you is one of lies and negativity and therefore the real matter cannot be resolved.

Speaking your truth changes things and enables everything to evolve on a more satisfactory level for you. So do not be courted by desire, do not allow yourself to be tempted and misled, for, as my grandmother used to love saying, "It'll all end in tears." Replace all the negative words like 'want' in your vocabulary with positive ones like 'need'.

Desire is a requirement coming from the five physical senses. They want instant gratification and they have seen what they desire either on the television, in a magazine, on the radio, or in the possession of someone else. Therefore they create a clamour in your mind, shouting, "I want, I want," and in order to silence this noise you go out and attempt to procure what it is that will give you respite from this ceaseless chatter. In contrast, need is something which you feel deep inside you, in your heart, in your very centre. You are aware of this yearning in a small way at first, but it grows and grows inside you until you realise that in order to be fulfilled you must take action.

The act of succumbing to one's desire comes from a different place to that of action taken to fulfil yourself. The former is a transitory action whereas the latter is a permanent action. Satisfying your desire will bring about a temporary respite from your physical senses, but because the action demanded by them is only shallow they will not be appeased for long. The need for fulfilment comes from deep within you, and thus, when you take the action it requires, your sense of fulfilment and the memory of it will stay with you and bring you happiness in the future. The desire, the clamour of which you have temporarily alleviated, will soon be forgotten along with the memory.

So you see that it is prudent and wise to invest in your needs because of the sense of well-being that is given to you in consequence, rather than in your desires, which are so transient and fickle.

The Beacon

How could this happen?
Where did it all go wrong?
Your love was like a shining beacon
Helping me through my day.

If I was floundering
Your light guided me safely home;
If I had been adventuring
It welcomed me back with my tales.

It was total, it was true,
The purest light there could be,
Always there, sending its beam to where I might roam,
Showing the way back to you.

And then one day you told me
That the beacon was no longer there.
It had faded away suddenly
Because there was no committed care.

Its bright and steadfast beam,
Sending its love vibration with confidence,
Had suddenly been beset by darkness.
It had simply ceased to exist.

But was it still really there
Hidden beneath its cloak of black?
Just waiting to be reignited
By a spark of love sent its way?

At first the spark met only darkness
However often it was sent;
But there was a strong belief known as trust
That something so beautiful could not die.

So day after day the love flew its course
Guided true from the heart.
There were times of grief, times of despair,
But trust was always there.

And eventually, only a matter of weeks
(Though at the time it felt like years)
The spark was reignited
And a weak light shone forth.

The dark cloak had been penetrated
And the chink of light was small, it's true;
However, the knowledge that it had not died
Kept the trust and love on course.

As each day went by the light grew stronger
The darkness it became less,
Until, finally, it shone forth in its former glory
A beacon of light for all to see.

The trust that this miracle could occur
Was what had maintained the belief it was not dead,
The love that was sent from the heart every day
Stirred the embers of what had been hidden.

Trust took the place of the beacon
While it was hidden from view
Guiding the steps each day
Giving security and upliftment in despair.

And now the beacon shines big and strong
Sending its light out across the world,
Welcoming me back from life's adventures,
Holding me steady in its beam.

But the light was more beautiful than before,
More clear, more special, more pure.
Both had grown from the experience
Knowing love and trust could conquer all.

Never again was complete commitment lacking.
The lesson had been learnt very well.
Together we journey through life's challenges
Upholding each with the beacon of the other's love.

Gift or 'Challenge'

Challenge is a dragon with a gift in its mouth...
Tame the dragon and the gift is yours.

Noela Evans

*R*elationships are the most complicated issues that any of us has to deal with, right from the moment we are born to the minute we die. Throughout the course of our lives we have personal and public relationships with a vast spectrum of people and they are the means of our growth. They are to life as textbooks are to exams.

Every relationship we have is either the gift of that person or a challenge to us from that person. We prefer the one who is the gift because it is so much easier for us to be with them. We enjoy their company, we can relax with them, and they are supportive and loving. However, because of our natural preference for the individual who is the gift, it is easy for us to underestimate what the challenging person is bringing to us. After all it is only in our perception that they are a challenge. What they are really showing us is what we need to learn about ourselves. They are a challenge because they push our buttons and make us feel angry, uncomfortable, irritated, ill at ease; all emotions that we would rather not have. However, if we realise that we are feeling like this because we have issues that need to be worked on, then we can be grateful to our 'challenge' and recognise it as also being a gift. Until we reach that space, the likelihood is that we will be unable to have such a deep relationship with them as with our gift.

My dad is my gift. I love him so much for all his love, support and teaching throughout my life. There is such a lot I would not have achieved if it hadn't been for his unflinching confidence in my abilities. My mother, on the other hand, is my challenge. Whereas my father and I always had a natural easiness in our relationship and enjoyed each other's company, I was always aware I could, without difficulty, say the wrong thing quite unintentionally and incur my mother's wrath. I often felt as though I was walking on broken glass when I spoke to her in case I said something inappropriate. A good way for her to make me behave was always to threaten to tell my father. The last thing I wanted to do was make him upset with me. It wasn't that she didn't love me or that I didn't love her. We did love each other. It was just that somehow we were on opposite sides of a swift-flowing river and neither of us could find the bridge so that we could cross over and be on the same side. If we could just do this we would miraculously be able to understand each other and speak the same language.

I was a rebel. Not deliberately. I just was. I had my own ideas about most things – what I should say, what I should wear, who I should be friends with, what I should do and so on. And I reacted against everything that my mother stood for. She was so attractive, always immaculately groomed and beautifully dressed with fingernails painted, and she graced my father's arm on every occasion. I used to think they made such a striking couple when they were going out together. I was the urchin who bit her fingernails, lived in jeans, refused to wear skirts and had long straight hair falling over my face. I hated wearing shoes, it didn't feel natural to me, so I would wear them when I left the house and then would take them off as soon as I was out of sight. But I got caught. One day my mother was driving down the road when she saw this barefooted girl. Imagine her horror when she realised that the shoeless child was none other than her own daughter. Was I in trouble that day!

My sister was her gift. She and my mother connected in the same way that my father and I did. She helped my mum inside with the cooking and the cleaning while I helped my dad work in the garden and carry out maintenance work around the house. I wished I'd been a boy because they seemed to have more interesting lives and more challenging future prospects. My sister was quite content to be a girl and adapted easily to making my mother happy. However, no one person is ever exclusively a gift or a challenge. My father and I gave each other challenges but because of the depth of our connectedness these challenges were much easier to deal with and learn and grow from than the challenges my mother and I gave to each other.

I grew up. I still bit my fingernails and worked in a predominantly male field. My mother was proud of my success but didn't understand me. I didn't understand her. We still hadn't found the bridge. My dad and I understood each other and continued to be close.

Then I had children. My first daughter was my gift. She was beautiful and loving and generally obedient although strong-willed. I enjoyed her company so much and as she grew older she understood me as I understood her. We were like my dad and I. We were on the same side of the river. And then I had my second daughter. Beautiful, content, quite happy to play on her own but, horror of horrors, as she grew older, not obedient! She was my challenge. Life had come full circle. To everyone else she was an angel, so well-behaved, so pretty and so polite. What a lovely child! They didn't see her when I was trying to get her ready for school. She and her sister would be dawdling. I'd shout. The older one would get ready, the younger one would stop. Eventually I realised that shouting had no effect on her whatsoever. In fact it did the opposite. The only thing that worked was me being patient and nice to her, which wasn't easy when she was running late for school. Then there was the choice of clothes. My older daughter would ask "What shall I wear, Mummy?", so I'd tell her and, good as gold, she'd go and put it on. Number two daughter would appear with two outfits, ask me which one she should wear and then promptly put the other one on. She insisted on wearing summer clothes in the winter and winter clothes in the summer. Dear Lord. What had I done to deserve this child? Then realisation struck me. She was behaving to me exactly as I had behaved to my mother. She wasn't deliberately being naughty; she was just being who she was. My older daughter was more like my sister; she was prepared to put herself out to be more amenable and loving. My younger daughter, like me, was living her truth with no compromise.

As she grew older I discussed with her the problems I'd had with my mother and how I didn't want to have the same situation with her. She agreed and for a short time we'd both try hard and then lapse back. We hadn't found the bridge. She was my husband's gift as my older daughter was my gift. I used to look on with amazement and wonder as they communicated and laughed with each other in a way that she and I couldn't, and question what I could do to change things. Years passed and my younger daughter and I stayed on opposite sides of the river. I allowed life to get the better of me and stopped living my truth. I went through a period where many things became distorted but as a result of all this I learned many lessons and grew.

My relationship with daughter number two was a carbon copy of the one I had with my mother. I felt as though I was skating on thin ice and any moment I could fall through. But then one day it dawned on me that this was a generational issue that had been passed down from mother to daughter for many years. Certainly I remembered seeing it with my mother, grandmother and great-grandmother. I realised that here was an important lesson to be learned and given all my other lessons I was now in a strong position to deal with this challenge. After all, what I was receiving was a direct mirror image of what I was giving out. So if I was creating this situation then I could change it.

I sat and meditated and realised that not only was this beautiful child my darling daughter who had grown in my womb and whom I loved dearly but she was also a symbol of me and how I'd felt when I was a child – hurt and rejected because my mother thought I was being naughty when all I was being was me. I recalled my mother had said something like that about her mother, and for all I know my grandmother had said something similar about her mother. So it had been passed down the line. There was also an element of the issue of control there: the adult not allowing the child to have her own way because the adult always knew best; the instruction for a child to always respect her elders, however her elders treated her. Having been given this awareness, I visualised myself as a young child. I then held her and felt strong outpourings of love towards myself. I held the child while the love soothed away the hurt and the rejection, until she felt safe, secure and loved, and then I brought her into my psyche and united her with me, as the adult. Since then my relationship with my younger daughter has gone from strength to strength. We are more loving towards each other, we enjoy each other's company and we laugh and chat a lot. It's wonderful. Finally I found the bridge, and I was the bridge. My daughter was showing me what I had to work on in myself. I was showing my mother what she had to work on in herself. Unfortunately, she didn't find the bridge this time. I am hopeful though, that by finding it, I will have broken the generational link, which will free up the past and future generations from this issue. The gift that my younger daughter brought me was invaluable. In these situations you always have to look at yourself, at the mirror image, to see what it is in you that needs to be changed, so that what is being projected, what is happening in the outside world, will also be transformed.

Some time ago I met a lady who was having exactly the same difficulties. She has never got on with her mother and she has always had difficulties getting on with her daughter. These issues are not uncommon but they are there to highlight what you need to work on and subsequently release within yourself. You always find the answer by loving yourself.

I have referred in detail here to family relationships and on observing friends' families I see it is true for them too. But friends, people we work with, anyone we meet during our day, can all be put into the gift or 'challenge' category. The gifts are the ones who embrace us and who we laugh with, who nurture and sustain us. Our lives would not be so rich without them. But the ones who are 'challenges' are essential to our growth and so it is important that we do not overlook their gift to us. This is why it is for us to learn to love ourselves unconditionally together with everyone else, be they gifts or 'challenges', for they respond to our needs, whether they are conscious or subconscious needs. The way in which they are behaving and reacting towards us, whatever it may be, is the lesson that we need to learn in order to free ourselves up from another of the pieces of baggage that we carry around. Without them behaving in the way that they do, as a mirror image, we would not be made aware of our need and would therefore be unable to grow and bring ourselves greater peace, love and contentment. By recognising and addressing what the other person is teaching you, you become empowered, which causes a shift in vibration between the two of you and removes the negativity you felt towards them. So these wonderful souls who bring us 'challenges' are actually doing us a great service, and when we look at it from this perspective we realise how right it is to love everyone unreservedly.

Loving oneself and others unconditionally is a very positive energy. It helps those who are struggling in the darkness, and it ensures that we stay in the light and do not attract any darkness to ourselves which will then need to be resolved. It is for this selfsame reason that we must always first and foremost love ourselves, so that we only send ourselves positive energies and not the negativity that occurs when we are continually criticising ourselves.

So, friends or family, strangers or acquaintances, gifts or 'challenges' who become gifts, all are to be greeted with love and a sense of excitement, because you do not know where meeting them is going to take you on your life's journey and what healing you are going to receive as a result of this.

All relationships are dual-sided because both parties attract what they specifically need to learn. As you progress along your pathway you recognise the other person as being a gift for they are bringing to you the gift of learning. Before you are on this pathway, however, you do not appreciate what the other person is bringing to you. You only acknowledge the irritation and the anger that they cause to you and in this way much negativity is born between the two of you. It is in recognising the gift that the other person brings that you can work through the learning that you need and then progress on your way as an enriched, enlightened human being.

Grief

Just an emotion like love and hate,
Happiness, sadness, laughter and tears,
But Grief is a black emotion.
It is suppressed and lurks deep in our psyche
Patiently awaiting its moment, when it surges
And knows release, freedom and in so doing causes more Grief.
It mutes the colours in our life,
It limits our ability to be truly happy,
It never leaves us
Unless we address it, deal with it
And say, the time is now,
We release you – be gone.
Grief is a necessary emotion,
A learning emotion, but it cannot be hidden.
In order to obtain the colours of Grief,
To change its hue from black to a rainbow prism,
It has to be worked through.
The memories have to be given space to remember,
The tears have to be given the opportunity to flow,
The full realisation of what life means without the other person
Has to be achieved
And then, and only then
Can the Grief be released,
And life's new challenges begin.
So do not fear Grief
Welcome it with open arms
For it is one of life's emotions
And is part of our soul's development and growth.
For we cannot experience what it is like to truly value someone
Unless we have experienced first the loss of another.

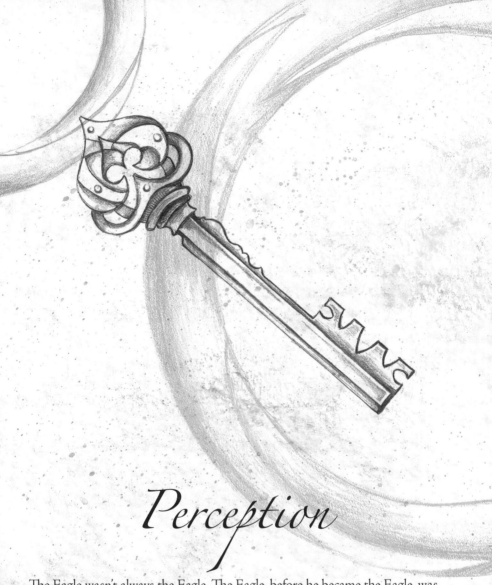

Perception

The Eagle wasn't always the Eagle. The Eagle, before he became the Eagle, was Yucatangee, the Talker. Yucatangee talked and talked. It talked so much it heard only itself. Not the river, not the wind, not even the Wolf. The Raven came and said "The Wolf is hungry. If you stop talking, you'll hear him. The wind too. And when you hear the wind, you'll fly." So he stopped talking. And became its nature, the Eagle. The Eagle soared, and its flight said all it needed to say.

Robin Green and Mitchell Burgess

*W*hat an all-encompassing, interesting word this is: *Collins English Dictionary* (3rd edition) states the meaning of 'perceive' as "to become aware of (something) through the senses esp. the sight; recognise or observe; to come to comprehend, to grasp." It then goes on to state that the meaning of perception is "the act or the effect of perceiving; insight or intuition gained by perceiving; the ability or capacity to perceive; way of perceiving; awareness or consciousness; view; the process by which an organism detects and interprets information from the external world by means of the sensory receptors."

Your perception is totally personal and unique, as indeed you are as a whole. You are a complex being made up of your genes and therefore traits of your ancestors, your own life experiences and what you have carried into this life from previous lives.

Your awareness sums up the entire way we see our world and the events that take place in it. Until shown otherwise, we presume everyone thinks the same way we do, and if they don't then we think they should. In other words we try to force our way of thinking onto everyone else whether or not we are right. When we decide to come back for this life the soul chooses the best set of circumstances for its learning. It chooses the family, or lack of it, the circumstances of the birth and the country, and so starts the beginning of the journey, the first step on the pathway of this incarnation.

The environment in which you are brought up has a strong effect on who you are, but so do your genes, which is why the genetic choice of parents is so important to give you the situation you need in which to learn. Your peer group is another body of people who can have a profound effect on you, as can your teachers. You may decide to agree with everything you are told, whether because you think you do in fact agree, you are fearful of speaking out against everyone, or you feel that the person who is telling you knows more than you do. Alternatively, you may be a person who disagrees either because you have to express what you know and feel, whatever the consequences, or because you like the attention you receive when you are being controversial.

The way that you respond to situations and are responded to as a small child colours your perception of the world and contributes to who you become. Your opinions are your security and when you meet someone who disagrees with you, you immediately feel threatened. There then transpires that considerable negative energy arises in the shape of anger, bitterness and bad feeling, and eventually one person becomes the victor and the other the victim. The victor will be seen as the strong one and the other as the loser, which will have ongoing repercussions. This is highlighted in *The Celestine Prophecy* written by

James Redfield. The spiritual adventurer in the book has learnt to see the energy fields around people when he concentrates. He sees two people having an argument and as he watches he sees that each time one of them wins a point the other person's energy is sucked into the winner's aura. Then when the loser makes a good comeback he gets his energy back along with the other person's. This is why after a fight, physically or mentally, the victor feels so good and the loser so bad – it is because the former has all the energy and the latter has lost all of his.

Consider all the disputes that have happened throughout history because one man's perception has differed from another's, including Holy Wars and clashes of fixed religious views, even today. All the wars have come about for the same reason: both sides think they are right and neither is willing to compromise. However, as we evolve it is time that we find other solutions instead of resorting to the negative energies that result in fighting.

We fight because we feel fear, because we think we may lose control; but consider the scenario if we are coming from a point of loving ourselves. Because we love ourselves we feel, and are, secure. It is not our perception of the world that makes us feel secure. The latter can be taken away from us, the former cannot, and therefore we do not need to feel negative about anyone else's comments. Indeed, if we were to acknowledge that the other person's perception of his world is just as real to him as ours is to us, we could sit down in our state of self love and discuss his point of view and see where we can both learn from each other and come to a mutually beneficial understanding.

Because humans have minds, which have a very strong voice, they generally listen to them, and disregard their instincts to such an extent that they become more and more muted, resulting in them moving further away from the lifestyle they are meant to have. All other beings on this Planet live according to their nature, their instincts and the seasons and continue in a harmonious, ecologically balanced way. Because we don't do this, we create increasingly negative energies and damage not only ourselves but also Mother Earth and every living thing on Her. It's not too late, however, to address this and resolve it by positive energies and by moving forward in our personal growth. The starting point of turning our whole lives, and subsequently the Planet's life, around is loving ourselves and then radiating this love out of us positively towards all other living beings, including the Planet, our Home.

If I was with a group of people and picked up a large stick and asked what it could be used for, the answers would be varied and would come from each person's perspective, their life's experiences. It could be used as a walking stick, to build a fire, to make a house or an item of furniture, or it could be used as a club to defend yourself or to murder someone. The stick itself hasn't changed at all – just the different perceptions. A whale can be seen as a wonderful creature of the deep from whom we can learn so much about the waters that cover most of our Planet, and also its way of life, its wisdom and knowledge; or it can be seen as a disposable commodity, to be killed and used for monetary gain. The ones who kill do not consider that the whales have any rights, despite the fact that they are living beings who inhabit the same Planet as us.

We know that we can wake up for no apparent reason in a really bad mood and, unless we do something about it, it will continue all day, colouring everything negatively, which in turn will make everything go wrong for us and put us in an even worse state. This frame of mind can be explained away as being the result of hormones, the weather, lack of sleep etc but ultimately we have to accept responsibility for it and acknowledge that we, and we alone, are capable of changing it. We can do this by filling ourselves full of self love, talking to ourselves as we would to a small child who has hurt itself and craves love and reassurance before it can continue with the next thing it has to do. For this is really what is happening to us. Deep inside, we are still the small child who has had the experience which has given us the perception we have had today and has caused our mood.

So when someone disagrees with you, don't feel threatened. Fill yourself with self love and radiate it out to the person who is being confrontational and then quietly, calmly and lovingly listen to what they are saying. Try and see what the learning is here for you, because neither of you is right nor wrong, you are merely coming from a different set of experiences. In this way it can have a very positive outcome. If you respond angrily to someone who is in dispute with you, all that happens is tempers flare, irrational things are said and the negative energies around you both increase. If, however, you respond in a positive way by listening and considering what is being said, and then putting forward your own point of view rationally, there should be a mutually satisfactory meeting place. Remember that people are only ever brought into your life for you to learn something from them about yourself, so by shouting at them and alienating yourself you are just making whatever it is you have to learn harder. It could be that they have come into your life to redress the balance of karma because of something you did to them in a former life. They are certainly there as part of your journey, giving you the opportunity to learn and grow if you choose to take it.

When your viewpoint is being challenged, listen very carefully to what is being said. Is it a fair comment? Is it justifiable? Where did your opinion come from? Is it something you really believe or is it the result of something your parents or someone else said to you when you were small, and subconsciously you've picked it up and made it your opinion? Is it right? Whatever your mother or father expressed as their opinions came from the place they were in at that time, from their perspective, which of course was also affected by the issues, experiences and ideas that they had subconsciously absorbed as they travelled their pathway. Make sure, therefore, that you always try to ascertain where your thoughts and ideas have come from. You know the old saying "Everyone else is mad, it's not me." This is so true. If you listen to someone talking about another person's situation they will interpret it exactly as they see it themselves, from their perspective, which is not necessarily the reality. If they are untrustworthy themselves, then they will consider everyone else to be the same. If they are always looking for a weakness in someone so that they can use it for their own advantage, then this is what they will see in others. So don't be drawn in by other people's perceptions and don't get upset by them. This is just another form of being judgemental – "I am right and you are wrong," and this is not the case.

I remember that many years ago there was a four-part series on television which made a lasting impression on me. I was probably in my teens when I watched it and it was about a family similar to ours, except that it comprised a mum, dad, son and daughter, whereas my family had two daughters and no sons. The first week showed a period of events from the father's point of view, the second week the same set of events from the mother's point of view, the third week the same set of events from the son's point of view, and the fourth and final week the same set of events from the daughter's point of view. Apart from very occasional overlap and the odd recognition of the events from a previous week, there was no resemblance to what they had done, thought or experienced. You would have thought that the whole series was describing four people with totally separate lives, who were not related to each other and were living in different parts of the world. This shows that all people, however closely they live together and whatever their relationships are, have completely different perceptions about the same events and look at things from differing points of view, depending on the level of importance that they attach to each occurrence.

It is so much easier when you no longer have to consider this aspect of life, because instead of feeling threatened when others disagree with you, you can see everything that happens to you as being part of a learning experience which you have attracted to yourself. Consequently you can grow to be more resilient and lead a happier and more balanced life, secure in the knowledge that however it may seem, disagreement is actually not a personal or intimidating attack on who you are – just a signpost and helpful assistance on your spiritual journey.

Perception is an ever-changing part of the human being. It can be rigid and fixed like a reservoir of water where there is no natural flow, or it can be like the waterfall where the stream has come down the mountain and then, with a tumultuous feeling of delight, leaps from the top of the cliff and down to the lower level where it continues its journey to the sea. When your perception shifts it is like the waterfall, for at the top of the waterfall you see things from one perspective but by the time you reach the bottom you see them differently. Without changing your state of mind, you would be unable to make the leap from the top of the waterfall to the bottom and yet this experience makes you grow and be more open to, and aware of, things that are in your life and in the lives of others.

You look at others with compassion, for you know that they are what they have created, that they are the people that they have to be in order to learn the lessons that they need to learn, and in being aware of this you feel love for them as well as for yourself, for you realise that their perception is no threat to you and that your perception is no threat to them, unless they choose to see it as such. Every time you choose to take the leap from the waterfall you will change and grow, and each time you will become more balanced as you continue your journey to your own ocean, which is your core, your soul, your truth.

Enlightenment

"Follow your heart" they said.
Good advice if you could hear what it was saying.
"To thine own self be true" I read
But the only way to do this was to "follow your heart"
And I couldn't.

"Why can't I hear what it's saying?" I asked,
But no one gave a reply.
I know I have a heart, but why isn't it speaking?
Or maybe it is and I'm deaf to its cries.

I knew it wanted to soar like the birds
In freedom, know total excitement,
I knew it wanted to dip and swoop
Like the sails on the boats at sea,
But I knew it couldn't.

And then one day the truth was revealed,
My heart was tightly chained.
So tightly chained it could neither murmur nor stir
And the chains were so big,
They were anchor chains.

With this realisation I understood
Why my heart had appeared to be dumb.
I had inflicted the pain, stifling the sound as it complained
Until it spoke no more.

Trying to keep everyone happy,
Be all things to others except me,
I put myself last, anything less would be selfish,
And so I succumbed to my programming.

The result was the slow downfall of my heart,
Its protests becoming mute.
I thought I had to live for others, not for myself,
Not realising in this the greatest selfish act I could make.

In trying to protect them
I kept them from the woven colours of life.
In trying to protect them
I prevented them from experiencing what was theirs.

But now, thank you God, my blinkers are gone,
I made the first step by telling the truth.
I felt the chains start to shift and gently break.
I stepped out with integrity and felt the chains fall.

And now my heart is healed and whole again,
A beautiful being that I shall always love,
A being that I shall always respect,
A being that I will never stifle again.

And so when they say "Follow your heart"
I shall;
For now it speaks to me loud and true,
And for my sake and others
I walk my path and enable them to walk theirs.

Forgiveness

To err is human, to forgive divine.

Alexander Pope

*F*orgiveness is the key that fits the lock to the door that keeps you imprisoned. By not forgiving another person who has hurt you, you are keeping the pain close to you, you are refusing to let it go, and the one that you are hurting the most as a result of this is yourself. By your refusal to forgive there is a cord of energy which still connects you to them and it is only through your forgiveness that this cord can be broken so that you are free to move on.

By forgiving someone I do not mean that you excuse their actions, but you can say "I do not agree with what you did/said to me, but as one soul to another I forgive you." You do not have to say it out loud to the person concerned; just say it to yourself in meditation, as you stroll along the beach, as you climb the hills, as you walk through the woods – wherever you feel most comfortable. It is amazing how liberating it is to say that and to feel the freedom as a result. You have carried all this hatred around inside you and it has been eating away at you, sullying everything that you touch and damaging everything that you do. You have possibly even reached the stage where it has become such a part of you that you do not wish to let it go. But believe me, I know from personal experience that it is an incredible relief when you let go and move forward. It's as though someone, somewhere has suddenly turned the light on for you and your life seems so much better, because you are no longer dragging this ugly heavy stone of hate around with you everywhere you go.

While you keep the hate inside you it acts like a poison, infiltrating your body, running along your veins and arteries, affecting everything that you do and spoiling your life until eventually it destroys you. We all know people who have allowed something that happened to them to ruin their life. And who has this benefited? Certainly not them. Even if you don't mean it, still say those words "I forgive you" because by just speaking them things will start to change for you and one day you will suddenly realise that you actually mean them.

To look at forgiveness in another context: your initial reaction is "I'm hurting," but remember that everything finds its own balance. If someone has hurt you then the law of energy (the law of karma) demands that the person who has done the hurting will receive it back, probably not from you at all but from some other source so that they can have the opportunity of learning what their actions have felt like to the person on the receiving end. Then if they learn at this stage the consequence of their actions, it will give them the chance to redress the balance and sort things out. So, while you are going through the thought process of whether to forgive or not, it is firstly most important that you realise that this is the best thing for you, and then take into account that whatever this person did will come back to them without you having to do anything about it.

I was once put into a very bad situation by someone whom I considered to be a friend. My grandfather, who had been my business partner, had recently died, resulting in several urgent matters to be attended to at work. We had two full-time secretaries and an assistant, who had all been there for some time. Suddenly, and unexpectedly, one day my secretary told me she was leaving for a job with better pay. I asked her where she was going and whether I could match the increase but she refused to tell me. She said that there was no way I could pay her the amount she was going to receive. I was upset, because she had worked with me for several years, but there was nothing I could do about it. Then, a few days later, the other secretary told me that she, too, was leaving. Within a matter of two weeks both the girls had left and there was just the assistant and I left to do our own typing. I was in a state of shock, because I could not understand what had suddenly happened to cause the annihilation of our happy office life. Then I found out that one of our competitors, whom I had known for several years, had poached both the girls. He and his business partner were setting up on their own and, knowing how good my secretaries were and how experienced they were, he came and saw them at their place of work, my office, and offered them a vast salary each. There was no way that either of the girls could afford to say no. There was also no way that his business could sustain such high outgoings. Although we were competitors in the locality where we worked, we all got on well together, and until now there had been no sharp practice carried out. It was a traumatic experience and I was very hurt by it.

But within the course of the next few months, without me being involved in any way, the Universe took care of things, the balance was redressed and he was exposed as the person he really was. I found a way of making my business more profitable with the new staff, who were just as efficient as the old ones, so it turned into a positive experience for me. If the original secretaries had stayed, things would have just continued in the same vein but their action of leaving caused me to look at the business in a different light. One of the girls rang me up and told me how unhappy she was and asked if she could have her old job back. Unfortunately, by that time I had already replaced her, so she ended up going back to the place where she had worked before she joined me. The other girl rang me up in a distressed state and asked me what to do, because she was being sexually harassed by her new employer. She ended up leaving. He was then imprisoned for fraud. I have found that this has happened all through my life: the Universe has always dealt with things in the correct, balanced way without my intervention. If I had tried to get my own back, I would have created an imbalance of negative energy for myself and would have been subjected to the law of karma. I always think that this is what is meant in the Bible when it is written "'Vengeance is Mine,' saith the Lord." Let the Universe deal with it, and that way the outcome will always be the right one for everyone to learn and grow.

It would not be in your highest and best interests to continue to judge the person who has offended you. Yet this is what you are doing by not forgiving them. You do not know what lessons they have come back to learn and what experiences they have had which have made them behave in this way. Therefore they may not have behaved correctly towards you but generally, if someone does something hurtful to someone else, it is because they are walking in the dark themselves, their lives are based on negativity and they are hurting inside. So by not forgiving them you are harming yourself and adding to the pile of negativity and darkness that they are already struggling beneath. By not being compassionate in this situation you are behaving to them in the same way they behaved to you originally, without compassion, and so that means that you are no better than them. The lesson for you is to turn the negative into a positive for yourself and trust that the Universe will correct the balance. It always does, even if it is not blatantly obvious to you. Do not dwell on it, let go and move forward.

Another good reason to forgive this other person is that, since we create what we need in our lives to learn from and to grow, we have actually created the situation which has caused us the pain. We needed another person to take whatever action was needed so that we could learn our lesson. If we choose to play the role of victim we have to have an oppressor. If we decide to be the person who is always in control we have to be with someone who allows us to do that. So in everything that we select, either consciously or subconsciously, for ourselves, there has to be another person involved to enable us to play the role that we have chosen. So whatever this other person has done to us it is because we created the environment in which it could happen. So again, instead of allowing your anger, pain, frustration and hurt to fester and grow, making you feel ill, bitter and unhappy, it is in everyone's best interests, especially yours, for you to be freed from this vicious circle of negativity by forgiveness.

Once you've forgiven the other person concerned – not condoned remember, only forgiven – then you can use all your concentration, thought and awareness to see why you created the situation. From this point will come about your realisation and your growth. After all, if you don't get to grips with your issue at this stage it will only keep happening, and each time in a more extreme way to get your attention, until you realise why. Therefore, if you can deal with it now and avoid going through the pain of a repeat performance, it is definitely the most loving thing you can do for yourself.

Initially, you may find it very challenging to see what it is that you are meant to learn from the situation which you have created, but if you sit and meditate and ask for guidance it will be given to you. It may come as a small realisation which is added to and continues growing, or it may be a huge "Eureka!" Some people get their answers from something that is said on the radio or the television that connects with their inner knowing. One person I know used to get their answers by reading vehicle number plates! However it occurs, you will be able to work through your challenge by addressing it and subsequently resolving it.

I never used to ask for guidance and even if it was given didn't recognise it as such. I regularly, metaphorically speaking, banged my head against a brick wall over and over again by repeating the same programming, until my head was hurting so much that I finally learned my lesson. Those days are over now, thank goodness, and I am far more 'tuned in' and aware of the reasons why certain things happen in my life.

Very often the hardest thing is finding the answer to the question "Why?" When you know, then you can start working on what it has highlighted about you. If you need help to work it through, then go and get help. Do not put it off. Do not delay. Remember you love yourself so much you want to deal with this matter in order to move on. Your life really is like reading an exciting adventure book. Each page has a new challenge but there is always a way to resolve it, because you have been given all the tools that you need. It is just a case of recognising the challenge and then addressing it.

It is perfectly natural to have emotions; indeed you would have great difficulty if you did not, because that would mean that you had suppressed them so deeply they would be causing you great physical and mental damage. Emotions are important markers for our learning process. It is right for us to acknowledge them and to say "I am hurt," "I am sad," "I am unhappy," "I am angry" etc, for by doing this you are speaking your truth and owning your feelings. But then it is important for us to move on and ask ourselves why we feel like this. It is never just the situation that has caused the emotion. A negative, emotional situation is the trigger for you to delve deep and remember how many times you have felt like this before, and then go right back to the first time, 'the seed pod', when something happened that made you feel this way. In working through this you will be instigating a natural healing process enabling this particular issue to be resolved.

There may be certain situations when, however hard you try, you just can't forgive the other person. Then try looking at the situation differently. See if you can discover what the whole experience has really been about, what learning is there for you and then, when you've discovered it and moved forward, you'll find it easy to forgive as you will be grateful for the lesson that you have been brought by the other person. There is no right way or wrong way, only the way that enables you to move forward.

When you start realising that everything that is happening in your life is because you have created it and you begin investigating the root cause of why it has occurred, you will realise that everything is a signpost to help you along your pathway. Every time you work through an issue you feel so much better, you stay in a positive mood for longer and you are much happier. Forgiveness of others gives you freedom from the tangled spider's web of dark cords, attaching you energetically to so many people that you have accumulated through your life and which continually drains you.

Forgiveness is the pearl on the floor of the ocean for you to find and to share with the world. It is rare, it is beautiful and it brings great happiness. When the art of forgiveness has been mastered it is not forgotten, for, when forgiveness is extended from the heart, it touches all who come within its sphere. It acts as a guiding light for others who have not yet learnt the art of forgiveness. They see how the person who does the forgiving walks with a lighter step and a bigger smile and a sense of great freedom as a result of the words that have been spoken from their heart to the one who has hurt them; for it is through actions that others learn.

So many times it has been said that actions speak louder than words. The words may be spoken by many but if the action is not taken then the words are meaningless. So it is the action that has the value and enhances the learning. So find the pearl that is waiting for you, collect it and keep it with you at all times so that when another situation, another challenge, arises on your life's pathway, you remember the pearl and place it in your mind's eye, on the heart of the person that you are to forgive. This will help free them from the negative effect of their action and will release you from the cause and effect syndrome. The love and the beauty and the light that radiate forth from this pearl will indeed help you to grow in your own light, love and beauty.

The Mistake

We made one mistake
That was all
But from that mistake others have grown
Now we are so enmeshed
Will we ever be free?
Will we be penalised forever
Because we made one mistake?

We made one mistake
Our excuses are many
We were young, we grew up in the 60s
We thought we knew it all
We thought things were going wrong
We didn't think that what we had was strong
And so we made one mistake.
We made one mistake

And now with hindsight
We see it clearly, we were wrong
We had it all
We had everything there could be
It was special for you and me
Is it too late
To rectify our one mistake?

The Decision

I sit here with tears rolling down my face.
At the other end of the house
A similar enactment is taking place.

Outside even though it is summer
The sky is grey and foreboding,
Echoing our feelings with its continual rain.

How can I leave a husband who is so good and true?
By all accounts I am such a lucky woman
What do I have to do to realise this?
In one destructive move I am ending his life,
Everything he has worked for, everything he holds dear.

I am separating not just us, but the children.
I shall not be living across the road
But the other side of the world.

I doubt my motives, my reasons,
I look deep into my heart again.
Will this be a decision that I shall always regret?

No, the answer comes back.

The pathway you are walking is your pathway
And you have to walk it alone.
Be guided by your instincts and your intuitive knowledge,
Know therefore that that is the only way to go.

Even though you may wonder why
And feel desperate sadness at the pain and hurt caused,
Know that even though this is an ending
It is also a beginning for all.

And when the hurt, the emotion and the turmoil have subsided,
Each one will know that the right decision has been made,
That their pathways have been altered
But for their greater happiness and knowledge.

So listen to your heart
Listen to your soul
And know that the only true pathway for you
Is the one to which you are guided and which you can choose
Knowing that it is right
And because it is right for you
So is it also right for all.

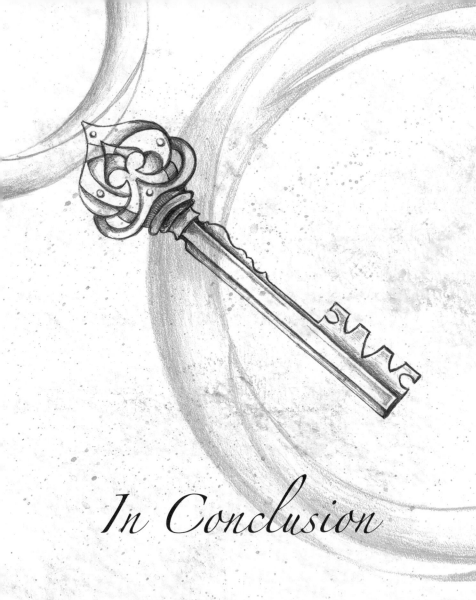

In Conclusion

Imagination is the beginning of creation. You imagine what
you desire, you will what you imagine and at last you
create what you will.

George Bernard Shaw

*T*his is the gift that I have been given and I share it with you. All truths are simple; it is living them that creates the challenge. Believe that you are walking your own pathway of life and that all the challenges which come your way are for your learning and growth. Because of your love for yourself none of these challenges are too great and you look at them in self love, trust and truth, and ascertain what it is you need to learn. It doesn't matter if you don't get it right first time; it is merely a learning experience and, having tried it one way, you can then undertake a different way until you have succeeded in gaining the knowledge you need. Ensure, however, that you do not place any pressure on yourself. This is not an examination that you have only three hours to complete; you have the rest of your life and future lives to get it right. But you will find that by trusting that everything is correct and not pressurising yourself, the answer will come to you. You can then progress along your pathway, having grown, and greet your next challenge.

I make no excuse for repeating some things in different chapters and not being able to completely segment our issues into neat little boxes, for this is not the way of our life. Each issue affects every aspect and colours our perception in all things. For our life is like the waves of the sea: every part of us rolls into the whole like the waves on the ocean. As we deal with our issues one at a time we see an immense clearing which enhances the whole of our life – not just one small area but every single part.

Always make sure that it is your dream that you are living, not someone else's, for their dream is not yours and never can be. They can live their dream in truth but for you everything will become distorted, for you will be living a lie, and in doing this you will attract your distortion back to you in order to get you to return to your pathway of truth. Therefore be honest with yourself, first and foremost, and then with everyone else. Live your truth and your dream for your own sake and for the benefit of all those around you. This you will do automatically if you love yourself, but if you are not in that space you will consider that you do not have any self worth. You will believe that everyone else's wishes are more important than yours and because you love them it is right for you to accede to their wishes. But this is not the case, either for you or for those that you love, for in living a lie this is the example that you set for them and then they believe that that is the way to live and they become dishonest to themselves, too, compounding both your challenges and theirs. Loving yourself first is the greatest gift that you can give, not only to you, but also to others, and in living this way you liberate yourself and everyone around you.

Walk in positivity, truth and trust, knowing that everything is right and as it should be and that every single thing that comes into your life is a lesson. Accept that everything in your life occurs in divine right order and for your highest and best good. Embrace all experiences and only allow positivity to flourish in your being.

Speak your truth in everything, for this way it will not only be right for you but you will also be helping others to confront their issues. I cannot emphasise strongly enough, however, that whenever you speak your truth it must always be said gently and with compassion, for truth never needs to be said aggressively or angrily, because it just is. When you are speaking your truth you are using a different energy because the words come from your heart and soul and not from your ego mind. If the person to whom you have spoken is uncomfortable, then that is their issue not yours. You will never need to force your truth down someone's throat. This is not a power struggle. It is simply who you are.

For as Nelson Mandela said in his inauguration speech in 1994:

"Our deepest fear is not that we are inadequate. Our deepest fear is that we are powerful beyond measure. It is our light not our darkness that most frightens us. We ask ourselves, who am I to be brilliant, gorgeous, talented and fabulous? Actually who are you not to be? You are a child of God. Your playing small doesn't serve the world. There is nothing enlightened about shrinking so other people won't feel insecure around you. We were born to make manifest the glory of God that is within us. It's not just in some of us. It's in everyone. And as we let that light shine, we unconsciously give other people permission to do the same. As we are liberated from our own fear, our presence automatically liberates others."